MW00896851

DISASTROUS INTERVIEWS:

The Comic, Tragic and Just Plain Ugly

by

Charlotte L. Stuart

Copyright © 2013 Charlotte L. Stuart
All rights reserved.
ISBN: 1492214663
ISBN 13: 9781492214663
Cover designed by Dana Sullivan

Table of Contents

Introduction:
The Finger Points the Way

It was my first interview after completing my M.A. There weren't many job openings in the area and I wanted to stay where I was, so I was both excited and nervous as I sped down the road in my Fiat 850 Sports Coup. I admit that I may have been a little heavy on the gas pedal, but the sun was out, it was a gorgeous day, and I was feeling lucky.

It was a two-lane highway, with lots of traffic headed in the other direction, but very little traveling in my lane. So when I found myself behind a conservative sedan that wasn't maintaining a constant speed and was definitely going too slow – both for road conditions and the speed limit - my irritation level quickly reached its max. Everything had been so perfect to this point. It took a long time before I got an opportunity to pass. When I finally did, I impulsively flipped the guy the bird as I flew by.

The interview with the team went amazingly well. When they suggested that I meet the Board of Directors immediately, I practically skipped down the hall in my high heels. Then, as I found myself being introduced to the first of the members of the Board, my engaging, interview smile froze in place. This was the very same man who had been driving the car I had zipped past on the freeway. The image of my raised finger hovered in the air between us like the disembodied digit of a shadowy apparition as he smiled back.

"We've already met," he said.

Disasters or Just Plain Ugly

The phrase, "*It was a disaster,*" is something I've heard many times when asking people how their interview went. I've also heard this same phrase from recruiters and hiring managers and have even uttered the words myself on more occasions than I care to remember. What does it mean when you categorize an interview as a disaster? Said with feeling, it's a way of rolling all three common dictionary definitions of the word into one:

disaster [dɪˈzɑːstə]
noun
1. An occurrence that causes great distress
2. A grave misfortune
3. *Informal* - A total failure

The cumulative impact of hearing this phrase so many times when chatting about interviews was one of the reasons for writing this book. The other was my own experience with interviews, especially my first professional interview. Amazingly, despite giving a board member the finger, I got the job. But the experience has stayed with me, indelibly etched in my life's book of stories. For what we keep from a bad, weird or stressful interview experience is a story, a story that we may or may not tell others right away, if ever. Sometimes we are embarrassed, sometimes angry, sometimes just frustrated. It may take a while before we can laugh at the situation and ourselves. But hopefully the healing force of laughter eventually arrives, bringing with it a sense of relief and the ability to let go and to move on. Even if we are occasionally plagued with a twinge of angst from memories of interviews past.

Collecting the Stories

Today, networking has become not only easy but a necessity. Between LinkedIn, Facebook, professional organizations, and people met in one context or another over the years, it doesn't take much to put together a list of emails of people in representative fields and organizations. That was how I began, by creating a very long list of names and compiling email addresses. Then, since I wanted to set a humorous tone for collecting the stories, I included the following explanation in the first round of emails:

Why did I receive this?
You are on this list because:
- *You are a friend*
- *We've worked together*
- *We have a group or friend in common*
- *I just happen to have an email address for you*

I wasn't sure I would receive *any* stories, but anticipated if I did, they would be humorous since I asked for "funny, weird or disastrous stories." I had no idea that more than half would be partly or totally serious. I thought those three words implicitly called out for the kind of story you tell over a glass of wine, or maybe a second glass of wine. But there is apparently something about living through a bad interview that reaches into the depths of our emotional lives, and when the opportunity presents itself, seeks the comfort of sharing. So share they did. The funny, the weird, the sad, the obnoxious, the triumphs and the failures.

Slowly my list of contacts grew as I managed to look up people from my past as well as getting referrals from those I had contacted initially. To my surprise, my network continued to expand as people who knew people who knew other people passed along my request for stories. Most told their story from the point of view of the interviewee, but many shared from an interviewer's perspective. At one point I noticed that there were themes emerging and decided that it wasn't the quantity of stories that was important, but the telling of similar experiences in a way that made them more palatable and possibly more of a learning than an ego-deflating experience.

One hundred thirty-four of the best of these stories are in this book, grouped around fifteen themes that evolved organically. Except for minor changes to clarify facts or chronology, the stories are essentially as told by the individual in first person. A few, however, are told second-hand by individuals who had been told the story by a colleague or friend. I received the majority of stories via email, some from telephone interviews, and quite a few from informal settings. One thing I discovered is that once one person shares an interview story in a group, others invariably open up and share their own experience.

The stories come from a variety of professions and include both management and non-management jobs. Some stories are funny; some are sad. Some are both funny and sad at the same time. Some are factual while others suggest lingering bitterness. Because of the range of emotions attached to their stories, the names of the contributors have been withheld. For the same reason, I have not named any of the companies, non-profits or government agencies that were identified in the stories when people sent them to me. You may think you recognize a few. It's hard to completely disguise large multi-national, highly visible corporations like Starbucks and Microsoft. But, at the same time, it seems unnecessary to know whether a story is about Target or Premera Blue Cross, a small technology start-up or a local company. A stressful interview is a stressful interview, and you can experience one in any organization of any size and in any business, and from both sides of the table.

In the end, what I discovered by asking people about their interview experiences is that if you have ever done a job search or conducted an interview, you probably have one or more stories that could be in this book.

Keep Calm and Carry On

The original "Keep Calm and Carry On" poster was created in the UK at the beginning of World War II to strengthen morale in case of a disaster. Currently, the slogan is used to encourage maintaining control in difficult situations. Thus, the slogan seems appropriate when talking about interviews which are frequently difficult and where both interviewees and interviewers aspire to maintain a semblance of control or calm.

As someone who has worked in a number of different professions – everything from teaching to commercial fishing in Alaska to management consulting – I can appreciate how difficult it is to make transitions from one job to another and to go through the stress of interviewing. And, as a manager and HR professional, I also understand what it's like to sit on the other side of the interview table.

Because I've experienced the full gamut of interviewing – created interview processes, conducted interviews, and been interviewed – I follow each story with my own comments labeled *Winning Moves*. Although some of the comments are fanciful observations linked to the themes, most try to capture the essence of the lesson learned from the experience. Then, at the end of each chapter, there is a section titled *Lessons Learned the Easy Way - Through Someone Else's Experience*. These are more specific recommendations based on the stories as well as my work in human resources.

In addition to the chapters that contain the stories, there are three chapters devoted to the complex and often confounding nature of the hiring process. Chapter One discusses the impact of the changing job market on the interview process. Chapter 17 focuses on the HR context and the metrics that influence the process from the inside, factors that increase stress levels for both the interviewee and the interviewer. And Chapter 18 overviews practical ways to cope with the aftermath of a bad or weird interview experience.

At the very end is an *HR Discussion Guide*, a list of questions specifically for HR professionals to use as a supplement to their orientation and training for those involved in the recruitment and hiring of employees.

Who should read this book? Anyone who has ever experienced a bad interview or who is worried about an upcoming interview. Anyone who has to hire people through the interview process. Or anyone who just likes to read about the misfortunes of others. Hopefully we can learn and grow from the experiences of others rather than having to learn everything the hard way.

Ultimately, interviewers and interviewees would be well served by the advice in the WWII propaganda poster: "Keep Calm and Carry On." Although I think some ranting and raving should precede the calm. This book strives to provide both the emotional release and suggestions on how best to "carry on." In reliving the stories from our interviews we can find solace, growth, and hopefully some snickers and belly laughs.

1

"I Coulda Been a Contender"

It sometimes seems like everyone else has a fantastic job with a salary to match. They travel to exotic places at the company's expense and get a year-end bonus to acknowledge their hard work and professional talent. While *you* are still searching for a job, preferably the ideal job, keeping track of your non-accomplishments while waiting for your big break. Of course you, too, usually put on your happy face when talking to acquaintances about work, so you know it isn't always easy to distinguish between "face" and reality. But in your heart you are certain that everyone else is doing better than you are, and that out there somewhere is the job of your dreams. One thing you know for sure, you definitely don't want to find yourself ten, twenty, thirty years down the line suffering from the Contender Syndrome, the feeling that you haven't lived up to your full potential. So you gird your loins (by summoning up inner resources, not by putting on a belt – though donning protective gear might be warranted) and go to yet another interview. Maybe THIS time…

The stories in this book illustrate not only the determination and resilience that interviewees display during sometimes long job searches, but the challenges faced by those on the other side of the table, the interviewers. In this chapter I take a look at the context within which the interview takes place – unemployment rates, the changing workforce, and common interview blunders and obstacles.

Slip Slidin' Away

Many of those currently employed as well as those looking for employment are worried about the present and pessimistic about their future, a future they may legitimately feel is "slip slidin' away." Those searching for jobs and preparing for interviews must deal with a mix of expectations, dreams, and harsh reality. Unfortunately, the ability to succeed in the job market is influenced by many factors, some of our own making, and some outside of our control.

Currently there are 86 million Americans actively seeking employment or thinking about changing jobs! Although the unemployment rate is at its lowest in almost five years, job growth is slow, and there are 7.9 million Americans who want to work full time but can only find part-time work. Downsizings, layoffs, and the Friday afternoon firings – all of these are contributing to feelings of disillusionment about the job market. Competition for existing jobs is fierce. In today's economy even finding an appropriate job to apply for can be difficult.

At the same time, it is estimated that as many as 52 percent of those currently employed would like to leave their jobs. In 2011 the Conference Board Review found that as many as 2/3 of U.S. employees are either actively looking for a new position or just going through the motions at work. And, unfortunately for the unemployed, it is conventional wisdom that it is easier to get another job if you are already employed. It may not make sense, but accounting for gaps in employment can be a very real obstacle in the job search process and pose some awkward questions during an interview.

The length of unemployment also has an impact on the strain of looking for and interviewing for a job. In particular, the 99ers - those who have extended their unemployment benefits for up to 99 weeks - may not feel as energized by a job search as they were when they were first unemployed. And the longer they remain unemployed, the more their skills become rusty and the more out of touch they become with the job market, their network, and the interviewing process.

Add to this already complicated mix the fact that the work environment is changing. In 1975 the average company was 58 years old. Today it's only 15 years old. Start-ups come and go. And so does the workforce. If the pundits are to be believed, even if you currently have a job, career employment is a thing of the past. We now spend about 2 ½ to 3 years in a job before moving on. That means that for the majority of us there are a lot of job interviews in our future!

Jenga Generations

Throw 'n Go Jenga is a game in which you roll a die to determine which color block to remove from a stack of blocks. You take turns removing blocks and adding them to the top of the stack until the tower falls. This is a little like what many organizations have been doing when replacing or adding employees in the workplace. Instead of rethinking the architecture of the tower, they continued to add more resources, expecting the same results. That is, until recently. Once Corporate America became aware that there are now *four* generations in the workplace, the generations have been labeled, analyzed, and sliced and diced from every perspective. Including the hiring and interview process.

Managing and recruiting people of different generations has been so thoroughly dissected that it has become an art form. The experts profess to know what employees from each generation want from a job as well as what motivates them both short-term and long-term. Thus, special questions for each generation of applicants have been developed to mirror what we think we know about them. Recruiters have created lists of questions that each generation's applicants might be expected to ask during an interview. This is considered especially critical for interviews with Millenials and Gen X, since Boomers and the Matures helped shape interview expectations of the past.

In the next ten years, it is estimated that up to 40% of the workforce will retire. At the same time, many retirees are returning to the workforce to make up for dwindling retirement savings. So the outlook for a more age-homogenous workforce is doubtful. Hiring and managing multiple generations will continue to be a challenge for organizations as well as for the job applicants themselves.

Is accommodating the different generations in the interview process a good thing? Does it give an advantage to a particular age group? Is it realistic to expect recruiters and hiring managers to know how the age puzzle will fit together in their teams? Are people really that predictable? I don't have the answers, but I know that these conundrums play themselves out in some of the interviews in this book. And not always in a positive way.

YOU can make the Top Ten

One time an HR friend called me from her office to ask for feedback. She had been told that there was someone waiting to see her that had made the comment that they were "under enough stress to kill ten people." She didn't want to be paranoid, but–. My advice was to take precautions. Fortunately, as we suspected, the woman in the waiting room thought that stress was killing *her*, not giving her a reason to kill others. Although not all stress is harmful, there are sufficient negative side effects to put interview stress on the map by including it on a growing number of lists.

Currently we can find the top ten for everything from "Most Courageous Dogs" to "Awesomely Pimped Out iPads" to "Non-profits Straight Outta Science Fiction." One list that's been around for a while is the Top Ten Stressors, and interviewing indirectly makes this list by foreshadowing a major life event or change. Interviewing is also a sub-set of two items on another popular list, Common Causes of Stress: "the inability to accept things as they are" and "neglecting to see the humor in situations." More significantly, psychologists cite the job search process as number four on the list of emotional events (tied with divorce). It's only a few ticks down from the death of a spouse, child or parent.[1]

When you think about it, interview stress *should* make top ten lists. After the hype of preparation and the adrenalin rush of participation, an interview, especially a bad interview, can be a real let-down. And the experience is often made worse by the second guessing and the uncertainty that follows. You might be angry at yourself or at the interviewers. Disappointed by your performance. Or upset about a missed opportunity. It's like failing a test in school, only more personal. If you don't get the job, they didn't choose you. They chose someone else.

---

1 Tony Bashara, Job Search Solution, (AMACOM 2006), p. 6.

Still another Top Ten category targeting interviewing is a list compiled annually by CareerBuilder.com. They survey HR professionals to find the "most outrageous interview mistakes" candidates have made during the year. This year's Top Ten list includes everything from the candidate asking the interviewer for a ride home to a guy who smelled his armpits on the way to the interview room. My personal favorite is the woman who is in the interviewer's office and asks the interviewer to leave her own office so she, the interviewee, can take a *private* cell phone call. I've also heard from HR colleagues about candidates who brought their mothers to the interview. And one colleague told me about a candidate who asked permission to go to the restroom during the interview and then failed to return.

What CareerBuilder calls an "outrageous interview mistake" might also be labeled a "disaster" or a "blunder." I like the word "blunder" because it *sounds* like a disaster. The Free Online Dictionary defines a blunder as *a usually serious mistake typically caused by ignorance or confusion* – take your pick. The blunders listed above are extreme examples of what a disastrous interview looks like, but there are other common mistakes that many job seekers make. According to CareerBuilder.com's survey, these include dressing inappropriately (51 percent), making negative comments about a current or previous employer (49 percent), appearing disinterested (48 percent), arrogance (44 percent), not providing specific answers to questions (30 percent) and not asking good questions when given the opportunity (29 percent).

The bottom line is that if you want to make one of the Top Ten lists, you have to be pretty darn creative, but almost anyone can commit a minor blunder. And from the interviewee's point of view, even a minor blunder can be a disaster.

Stressed is desserts spelled backwards

A palindrome is a word that must mean the same thing written in either direction, but a semordnilap (palindromes spelled backwards) is a simple text reversal that results in a valid word – like stressed and desserts. Some argue that there needs to be still another label to describe words that are not only valid when spelled backwards but that share some other connection. For example, "stressed" people often turn to "desserts" for consolation. *I'm feeling stressed – please pass me the chocolate!* And since researchers have found that dark chocolate may have health benefits, stressed out people can feel good about seeking solace in chocolate, or at least less guilty.

However, not everyone who experiences a disastrous interview turns to chocolate as an outlet for their frustration. Some go online to air their grievances on public blogs, including blogs targeting specific companies. For example, the following is typical of what appears on a blog devoted entirely to a warehouse distributor of home and construction products (a company that shall remain nameless, in this book at least):

What a joke. The online application was unbearable. First, they want your S.S. # and your DOB, why they need this information before anyone even speaks to you is a mystery to me. Their online application features an 85-question "personality test" that's idiotic even by personality test standards. I finally received a call from one of their HR people, a bunch of basic perfunctory questions and a "we'll let you know" which never happened. What a waste of time.

In return, interviewers get their revenge by posting stories about what ridiculous things candidates do, including the following online rant about resumes:

* *Candidate attached a letter from her mother.*
* *Candidate's hobbies included sitting on the levee at night watching alligators.*
* *Candidate explained a three month employment gap by saying he was getting over the death of his cat.*

Initially I thought both sides exaggerated…until I started reading the stories sent to me. Most came from people I knew to be sane and rational individuals who had simply experienced corporate America at its worst. Some had screwed up or blundered on their own. Which doesn't feel any better.

But no matter which side you are on when the disaster occurs, there is much that isn't pretty or palatable about a lot of interviews. Unfortunately, there are some things that even chocolate can't resolve.

The Optimistic Pessimist

The idea that we are supposed to accept adversity with a brave smile and strive to succeed in spite of all odds is played out again and again in television programs, movies, self-help books, sports, novels and even music lyrics. The concept is so prevalent that it often feels as though our response to disappointment or failure is scripted by our culture. But we don't have to follow the script. Personally, I'm drawn to the philosophy expressed by Despair Inc. that encourages us to "skip the delusions that motivational products induce and head straight for the disappointment that follows," but I understand the need to cling to hope. And, although I may rail against the idea that my attitudes are at least in part the product of the culture in which I live, I do try to keep a stiff upper lip when things go wrong. It's the mentally healthy approach to living, or so I'm told … again and again and again.

On the other hand, not everyone puts a smiley face at the end of every email. In Barbara Ehrenreich's book, *Bright-Sided*, she sets out to debunk the promise of positive thinking and argues that putting a positive spin on everything can result in self-deception and disappointment. At the same time, she acknowledges that being pessimistic is not the answer either. Rather, she encourages us to see things "as they are," as "uncolored as possible by our feelings and fantasies." [2] This is a mindset that is particularly helpful when dealing with the disastrous interview. Instead of putting on rose colored glasses to see you through a stressful interview, you may want to adopt what Ehrenrich calls "defensive pessimism" or anticipating and being prepared for "dire possibilities." By keeping a firm grip on your critical thinking skills, you can avoid swinging too far toward overly

---

2   Barbara Ehrenreich, *Bright-Sided* (Metropolitan Books, 2009), p. 196.

optimistic or the opposite, demoralizing pessimism. Who knows, you may even be able to eventually see the humor in what happened.

Interview Stories – The Good News?
They Happened to Someone Else

The next fifteen chapters of this book develop the themes I discovered when compiling and categorizing the stories sent to me. Some will seem familiar, others may not. But there is a thread of pain blended with humor throughout.

Sit back and enjoy. Unless you were on my email list, all of these interviews happened to someone else.

2
Humor is Like Pizza

Squid, pickled ginger, minced mutton, sauerkraut and pineapple, Spam and Kim Chi – there's a pizza topping for every taste bud. Similarly, humor takes many forms. There are chortles, giggles, belly laughs, guffaws, snickers and chuckles. Laughter can be wheezy, embarrassed, polite, forced, fake, and seductive. Then there is the manic, sarcastic, caustic and derisive. Not to mention the open mouth laugh with and without spittle as well as the mouth-clamped-shut-with-pinched-lips of the person trying hard not to laugh. Whether it's pizza toppings or laughter, there is enough variety to please the most refined palate.

It is estimated that children laugh as often as 300 times a day as compared to adults at 17 times a day on average. You can add some laughs to your daily quota by reading the following interview stories from people who not only found humor in their situations but were willing to laugh at themselves. You may choose your own brand of laughter to fit the story.

"'O frabjous day! Callooh! Callay!' He chortled in his joy."
Jabberwocky by Lewis Carroll

Several of the stories in this chapter are told second hand. The reason for this is the one thing all of these stories have in common – they are all seen by the narrators as funny. Whether laughing at their own situation or at someone else's, these are undoubtedly stories they've shared with friends and colleagues. Now they are sharing them with you.

One minor problem

"A Store Manager at a large discount retail store once told me about the time they interviewed a person, loved them, and were going to call them the next day to offer them the job – but changed their mind when the potential employee got busted for shoplifting on the way out of the interview."

WINNING MOVES:
Hint: Wait for the employee discount.

Go with the flow

"The recruiter met me at the door and was very encouraging and pleasant. Then when I entered the room, I was surprised to see a closed square of tables with people seated at chairs around the outside and one empty chair in the middle of the square. I was aware of a giggle or two as someone gestured toward the chair in the middle and invited me to take a seat.

Without giving it a second thought, I sat on the table, swung my legs over to the other side, and sat down. By the frown on the recruiter's face I knew that she was not happy with the set-up. I suspected that the interviewing team had come up with this on their own. She quickly made them open up the square and had me move my chair to the outside of the table at the front.

At that point I was feeling pretty good because I felt like I had passed the first test. Everything went just fine until I stood up and went to the whiteboard to create a chart to illustrate a point I was making. Again, I heard a few giggles and realized that I had reversed the information on the chart. I laughed and told them to look at it backwards and continued with my explanation.

It was definitely one of the stranger interviews I've had, but I liked their light-hearted approach, and they apparently liked how I handled myself. I got the job."

WINNING MOVES:

This story reminds me of a quotation from a book that has nothing to do with interviewing, although the sentiment seems apropos.

"If you just go with the flow, no matter what weird things happen along the way, you always end up exactly where you belong." Tom Upton, *Just Plain Weird*

Of course, acting impulsively can backfire. Just as playing it safe can be viewed in a negative light. It's a gamble either way. The real issue is whether or not you appear comfortable in an awkward situation. Not overconfident or cocky, but comfortable. And if you make the wrong choice for a particular group, perhaps in the end you *will* "end up exactly where you belong."

More than just a three-piece suit

"It was the spring of 1981 in New York City. I was 30 years old and had just found out that the Federal funding for my education project involving artists and special students in the NYC public schools was being yanked. So I needed to find work right away.

I had recently discovered that I had a somewhat exceptional mind for numbers, so when I saw an opening for an accounting job, I tossed my name into the hat. 'Accountant' - I could already hear the hoots and hysterical laughter coming from my friends.

Being an observant fellow, I noticed that New York City business types, including accountants, were conservative in dress and manner. Three-piece suits and stiff-collars. As a West Coast transplant, I was by nature more relaxed in dress and much more liberal in manner. But when in Rome....

I arrived at a nondescript mid-rise building in midtown Manhattan with fifteen minutes to spare in what I assumed would pass for full accountant drag. So far, so good. My first clue that this wasn't your typical NYC business was the unadorned waiting room, painted floor to ceiling in flat black with indirect lighting. The walls were angled, and there was no furniture. Hmmm.

The help wanted ad I'd spotted in the *New York Times* hadn't contained any description of the nature of the business, and the name of the company hadn't come up in my initial conversation with an unknown voice on the telephone. I had hoped to pick up clues when I got there - an annual report on an entry table, a proudly framed mission statement hanging on the wall, the company logo plastered everywhere. Any of these would be helpful for the initial interview. (West Coast quick adapter, right?) But other than the casually-dressed receptionist who gave me a head-to-toe once-over (was that a little twitch of a smirk on her face, or was I imagining things in the dimly lit room?), I still didn't have a clue as I was ushered into another small, black room.

My collar was getting tighter, the room smaller, and my prospects dimmer when a dis-embodied head entered stage left. It floated across the room with its closely shaved face, ultra-chic black eyewear, and a wry smile. My initial shock wore off when I realized that the head was actually attached to a very thin body clad in black from turtleneck to cap-toed shoes.

We exchanged very brief pleasantries, and then got down to the business at hand. The interview, lasting approximately fourteen seconds, went like this: a pair of deep blue eyes set in a disembodied head gazed at my slightly receding hairline, traveled ever so slowly down past my cheap eyeglass frames and my 1960s era dark brown mustache, to the starched white collar centered with a slightly crooked, Windsor knotted rep tie, past the gray pinstripe jacket, the cheap reversible belt (black out, brown in) more pin stripe and, finally, to my highly-polished wing tips. When the eyes rose slowly again to meet mine, I knew it was over.

I could have protested. I could have cried out that an entirely different person resided within the monkey suit, that I'd been on the leading edge of every artistic, musical and environmental movement since I was fourteen. And that working for MTV was a perfect fit. Instead, I said, '*Thank you so very much for your time.*'"

> **WINNING MOVES:**
> When you really need or want a job, you have to face the question of how far you will go to appear to be the person you think they want. Although in this case, the problem wasn't "fit" but not taking the time to find out more about the job before the interview. On the other hand, if it hadn't been for the Windsor knotted rep tie, he might have had a chance.

Right this way, please

"Our campus building can really be chaotic at times, with individual students and groups coming and going throughout the day. One time we had a group interview scheduled. The applicants were asked to assemble in the lobby and were told that we'd then escort them as a group to the interview room. Right before the interview was scheduled to begin, one of our staff went to the lobby and took role, calling out names and checking them off the list of interviewees. Everyone was present so the staff member asked them to wait one more minute while he made sure all of the interviewers were in place before bringing in the applicants.

A few minutes later, after ensuring that everything was in place, the staff member returned to the lobby and asked everyone there to follow him to the interview room. He did not realize that, in the meantime, another person had entered the lobby, and, in heavily accented English, had asked the front desk attendant where she should go to take her English as a Second Language (ESL) oral exam. The attendant had instructed her to wait in the lobby until he found out the location. Shortly after she took a seat, the interview staff member asked the interviewees to follow him, and the ESL student followed the group into the interview room and sat in the back corner.

One by one, the applicants were asked to stand and introduce themselves and tell the group why they were there. After the final interviewee gave her response, the poor ESL examinee introduced herself and explained, in trembling, broken English, that she was there to take her final English test. Initial laughter turned into applause from the entire room.

She was then escorted from the interview room and into the test room, where the instructor rewarded her with a passing grade for the presentation she had just made in front of the interviewees."

WINNING MOVES:

We sometimes laugh at the expense of others not because we are unkind, but because of the strange or unusual nature of the situation. Although it is easier to laugh at the predicaments of others, there are lessons to be learned about not taking what happens to *you* all that seriously. Turn them into stories and move on.

Great pecs

"The job interview that set me on my career path wasn't terribly auspicious. I was working as a nighttime typist alongside four guys, one of whom I had a slight crush on, even though I knew he was gay. Okay, perhaps I actually had a crush on his pecs. Anyway, he knew I was a bit of a techie and asked me if I was interested in an internship with a documentary film editor. (At his day job he was the documentary film director's assistant. Actually, we were all something else at our day jobs.) I thought about it for a second or two and then said, '*Sure, why not.*'

My day job was as a jeweler's apprentice. I got permission to take a couple of hours off for the interview, but there was a bit of a problem with how I would be dressed. The jeweler's shop was quite industrial which suited my basic Seattle grunge look just fine. But the internship was in Soho, so I was prepared to wear a nice white shirt under a grubby sweater and simply remove the sweater before the interview.

I remember knocking nervously at the film office door. It was answered by the gay guy with beautiful pecs and his good friend, an amazingly stylish, beautiful, blond woman. I came very close to saying, '*Hi, I'm short.*' After all of that worry about what I was going to wear, I left my grubby sweater on, feeling the need for as much protective body armor as I could get.

Thank god the director who interviewed me was neither tall, blond, nor an owner of impressive pecs. In fact, he looked a bit like a grunger himself. I sat very still as he looked over my resume. He got to the bottom of the page and saw that in college I had earned a specialization in film. He looked at me and asked why I hadn't gotten a film job after college. (I'd graduated a couple of years before.) Without a pause, I blurted out, with some feeling I should add, '*No one makes a living in film!*'

It was one of those moments when you realize you've just revealed your own stupidity in the most embarrassing way. Here I was telling someone who ostensibly made his living making films that it wasn't possible. Without missing a beat, he responded - with some feeling I should add – '*Well, maybe not in Seattle!*'

In spite of my inane comment, I got the job."

> **WINNING MOVES:**
> Just as there are no "stupid" questions, there are no "inane" comments — unless you are on the receiving end. Unfortunately, saying something you instantly regret is not uncommon in an interview. The key is to just as quickly forgive yourself and not let it ruin the entire interview. One of the biggest mistakes is to get caught up in a defensive explanation, making things worse and worse, when a simple, "Let me rephrase that..." will usually suffice.

Punch line

"A client of mine applied for an Executive Assistant job and decided to be creative during her interview by delivering a short PowerPoint presentation to highlight the reasons why she'd be a great fit for the job. The last slide delivered her punch line:

'And the final reason to hire me: I'm old, overweight, and the CEO's wife will never be jealous he's spending so much time with me!'

I almost fell off my chair with that one. Sadly, she came in 2nd – an internal candidate beat her out – but they said they LOVED her spark and creativity."

> **WINNING MOVES:**
> In this instance, there may not have been anything more the candidate could have done to get the job. But she is to be commended for making her presentation memorable. Perhaps if the CEO's wife had been a voting member of the recruiting team–.
> *"Creativity is the power to connect the seemingly unconnected."* William Plomer

Beans for lunch

"A senior HR Director was looking forward to meeting a very promising candidate for a particularly difficult to fill position. He had his usual lunch at his desk and just finished in time for the 1 pm interview.

There was a knock at the door, and the candidate walked in. As the HR Director rose to meet him he simultaneously and involuntarily let off a series of 'botty coughs' (British slang for 'bottom burp' which is slang for 'fart') completely audible and inescapable. There was no way to pretend it hadn't happened. With great shame the HR Director said, *'I must apologize for that. All I can say is that I will never have beans for lunch again!'*"

WINNING MOVES:

As the candidate, what is the correct response in this situation?

"Oh, no problem, it happens to me all the time."

"Oh, you had beans for lunch? They are very healthy."

"I didn't hear you fart."

"Solving the world's methane shortage, are we?!"

This is a tricky situation. Making a joke could make matters worse. But you have to acknowledge the apology in some way before moving on. Maybe with a head nod or a short statement such as: "I understand" (if you can say it without snickering). Then proceed with the business at hand.

Mud slide

"It was my first 'real' job interview with a budget office in a State agency. My past jobs had been babysitting and summer camp counseling. Getting this job as a sophomore in college meant I wouldn't have to beg my parents for spending money. I wanted it.

The agency was renting some buildings on my college campus. Since I was a resident there, I knew all the trails through the woods and could easily walk to the building where my interview was scheduled. Feeling pretty sure of myself, I took a short-cut on a dirt path. Then it happened… I slipped, feet flying up, tail falling down, right there in the middle of the trail.

When I got up and assessed the damage, I could see that the entire right side of my butt and half way down my right leg was completely covered with mud. Panic set in when I glanced at my watch and knew I didn't have time to run to my dorm room to change. Luckily for me, the coat I was wearing just barely covered all the mud.

My potential boss greeted me at the door and asked immediately if I wanted to put my coat on the hangar. I quickly said 'no, thank you' and gripped my coat a little tighter as if I thought he was going to forcibly take it from me.

As the interview progressed, I got increasingly hot. Not only did I have nerves because I wanted this job, but the temperature inside was unbearable. I began to sweat.

The interviewer must have asked me at least another two times if I wanted to take off my coat. The sweat glistening on my face must have seemed incongruent with my 'no, thank you' response.

The only other question I remember from that interview was '*Can you add?*' I answered, '*Yes, I can.*' It was a budget office and my position would be assisting a senior budget analyst with spreadsheets and simple input into mainframe systems, so I knew that was the correct response. I was so preoccupied by my embarrassing muddy backside and the oven-like heat that I have no clue what else he asked and how I answered.

In the end, I was offered the job. I never told anyone there about my 'mud slide.' That may not have been a good strategic move, however, because my boss frequently asked me about why I wasn't wearing my coat all the time. I think he knew–."

> **WINNING MOVES:**
> In this instance, Hugh Prather sums the situation up beautifully:
> *"Ideas are straight- But the world is round, and a messy mortal is my friend. Come walk with me in the mud..."*

Fail fast

"After the Columbine school shootings there was a push to re-think and re-train how police and SWAT teams deal with situations wherever there are a few bad guys and lots of good guys all mixed together. Before then, SWAT teams were usually called in when the bad guys had already been isolated. My company got a contract for work with an inter-agency group to put together training to better equip police and SWAT teams to deal with these situations. One of the reasons we got the contract was that we already had two former Navy Seals working for us. But we wanted to hire one more with more recent training and weapon certifications.

On the day of the interview I picked him up at the airport. He was a big guy, 6'5", about 225 lbs., lean, and strong looking. He had a gruff voice and talked with crisp, short sentences. I took him back to the office, introduced him around, and then took him into my office for a private conversation.

Once I completed my questions, I asked if he had any. He pointed to a sign on my wall that referred to innovation coming from 'failing faster' and said, 'What the f... does that mean?' I explained the need to prototype quickly and that in order to succeed you can't be afraid to try things. Sometimes you fail, but then you know what to do the next time. While I was talking he never blinked; he just stared at me. Nothing seemed to be registering. But he seemed like a good person for the job, so I hired him.

Later that month I went on a business trip. A week later I went to my office, unlocked the door and went inside. There was a KA-Bar knife stuck in the middle of the innovation sign. Our new employee had been on the job for three days. I went into his office and asked: 'You trying to tell me something?'

'I think I was pretty clear,' he replied.

I left the knife where it was. The guy worked the life of the contract. He was a super employee."

WINNING MOVES:

Pundits say that the faster we move and learn through failure, the faster we find a way that works. It reminds me of a Japanese proverb: *"Fall seven times, stand up eight."* Unfortunately, only failure is guaranteed.

Conclusion:

According to humorist and author, Gerry Hopman: *"Humor is like pizza, even when it's bad, it's still good."* This is especially true when it comes to interviews that happened to someone else. But it's even true of the funny things that happen to us...if we are willing to laugh about them. My advice is to fill your daily quota of humor any way you can. After all, laughter has fewer calories than pizza.

LESSONS LEARNED THE EASY WAY
(Through Someone Else's Experience)

Sense of Humor: You can choose to laugh at what happens or engage in a downward spiral of doom and gloom that will make it even harder for you to go to your next interview.

- *Turn bad interviews into light-hearted stories.*
  When we are able to find the humor in a bad experience, it makes it easier to cope and move on.

- *Research the company before the interview.*
  Almost all companies have websites these days. And there may be blogs or other online resources that can help you prepare. You may think it's a practice interview because it isn't your dream job, but if you don't prepare, it isn't even good practice. If you are offered a job you don't want, you can always politely turn it down.

- *Don't beat yourself up if you say something stupid.*
  A decision not to hire someone is seldom made based on a single comment. Most hiring managers look at the total package a person brings to the position.

- *Don't beat yourself up if you do something stupid.*
  Making a mistake when drawing a chart on the whiteboard. Passing gas. Having a stain or spot on your clothing. Everyone knows that sometimes things go wrong. The key is to demonstrate that you have the confidence to take things in stride. Of course it is easier to do in some situations than others. Which brings us back to the first point: *turn bad experiences into stories.*

3
Culture 2.0

At 10:22 am on June 9, 2009, "Web 2.0" officially became the English language's one millionth word. The term crossed over from technical jargon into wide circulation as symbolic of new ways of information sharing, networking and collaboration in virtual communities. At the same time, the concept of culture was evolving to keep pace with these technological changes by exploring diverse possibilities for interaction in a digital age. Thus "culture 2.0" was born.

Although company culture has never been static, the technology based culture 2.0 seems to enable and encourage more rapid and sweeping organizational changes than in the past. The flavor of the month may end up being the flavor of the week, evaporating as quickly as a fallen snowflake. But even when the change sticks, it's not surprising that it sometimes takes a while before the stories, collective experience, attitudes and behaviors of employees catch up to a new reality. Nevertheless, most recruiters and job candidates are looking for a good cultural fit and assume that this can be determined during the interview.

Recruiters are usually quick to tell applicants what the organization's culture is like, but it's like trying on clothes and only looking in the mirror from the front. What you need is the ability to check it out from multiple angles. Otherwise, you are "seeing" the culture like the blind man who encounters an elephant. Fortunately, there are usually clues during the interview that tell you what the culture beyond the brochure version may be like. And in some instances, the whole elephant can suddenly appear, despite attempts to keep it out of sight!

Not all of the following stories resulted in the person being interviewed actually landing the job. But in each instance, the question of culture "fit" is central to what happens in the interview - from arguing about the definition of culture to rejecting a position because of its culture to being rejected because you aren't seen as a good match for the culture. Whether we can describe a company's culture accurately or not, we are all sensitive to what we consider to be clues to what it would be like to work in a particular organization.

Culture war

"Most telephone interviews are pretty cordial affairs. The interviewer is usually an HR professional with a list of preliminary screening questions. As an interviewee your goal is to communicate your qualifications for the position and avoid saying anything incredibly stupid. And even if you are talking to someone higher up the food chain, the rules of engagement for the telephone interview are pretty standard.

That's why I was surprised to find myself in an argument over the definition of 'culture' on a telephone interview. It's one of my areas of expertise and, although I understand that perspectives can vary, the basic definition of what constitutes a culture is fairly standard. However, the person interviewing me didn't like my answer. She came back with: '*You are telling me how people communicate, not what the culture IS.*' I tried several times to clarify what I was saying, but I couldn't make any headway. She had me on speaker phone and I could hear her pushing buttons. Finally I suggested that this wasn't going to work and that we should end the conversation.

'*Why?*' the interviewer asked, sounding truly puzzled.

Since we didn't agree on the definition of 'culture,' I could hardly say it was a bad culture fit…"

> **WINNING MOVES:**
> The most common definition of culture is that it's a collective pattern of behaviors, values and unwritten rules that drive "how we get things done" in the organization. It seems to me that this story tells a lot about the organization's culture, even though the interviewer and interviewee didn't agree on a definition. In addition, this interview illustrates something valuable for everyone to remember: culture fit is a two-way street.

Wrong answer!

"This happened during the last of a series of interviews. I had been recruited to apply for a job – the first time this had happened to me. The company involved was a well-known, up-and-coming, interesting organization that produced video games, so I was very flattered to be asked to apply. As the process progressed, it was suggested that I visit some of their stores in the area to get a better feel for their business. It seemed like a good way to prepare myself for the next interview, so I made the tour, staying in each store long enough to get a feeling for their products and their customers.

When I arrived with my recruiter for the interview, it appeared that I was 'the' finalist. Everything went swimmingly. I even managed a few incredibly insightful and witty responses to the questions asked by the hiring manager. They introduced me around and showed me the office where I would be. Then we – the hiring manager, my recruiter and I – went back to her office and sat down to discuss specifics. This was the moment I had been waiting for: the offer.

Then something I wasn't expecting happened. The hiring manager leaned back in her chair behind her well-polished wood desk and asked: '*So on a scale of 1-10, how do you feel about the position at this point?*'

I knew the right answer. And I knew I should be looking at her instead of staring at the painting of a sailboat on the wall behind her desk. Everyone was silent, waiting. '*Seven*,' I said finally.

Wrong answer!

What happened next is a little foggy. I think there were mumbled comments about getting back to me. But I do remember the look on the recruiter's face as we stood in the parking lot. '*What was that all about?*' he asked, not even bothering to hide his frustration. '*I'm sorry*' was all I could say.

At first I was just mad at myself. I could have said 'no' after being offered the job. That way I could have come up with a face-saving reason. But the bottom line was that at the back of my mind, I knew that I didn't value the company's product, and that what I really wanted was to work for a company where I would be proud of what they did. Realizing this changed my career goals, so I thank them even though I'm sure they don't thank me for the experience."

> **WINNING MOVES:**
> When you are seriously looking for a job, it can be very difficult to face the possibility that the position you are interviewing for may not be a good one for you. Especially if you've been looking for a long time. But at the point at which you realize it would not be a good fit, you owe it to yourself to take the advice of the old Turkish proverb that states: "*No matter how far you have gone on the wrong road, turn back.*"

The following interview story is told by two different individuals. The first person was involved in both the termination of the person who held the position previously as well as being an interviewer for his replacement. The second part of the story is told by the person interviewing for the replacement position. Thus we are learn about the history of the position and a little about the concerns of the interviewers, the story behind the story, before we witness the actual interview through the eyes of the successful candidate.

Circumstantial evidence

The context

"I was a board member for a group representing commercial fishermen. Commercial fishing is a tough, physical job. Most fishermen are up at dawn and still at work after the sun goes down. It is not surprising that fishermen value hard work and expect others to put in a serious effort to earn their wages. So when another board member dropped by to talk to the manager of the group at his home office, he was surprised to find him in a robe and slippers at 10:00 in the morning. The board had already discussed their concerns about whether the manager was doing a good job, so when he related the details of his visit back to the rest of us, that was the end. The position was open shortly thereafter.

When the time came to interview candidates, we carefully prepared our questions and agreed to follow our process to the letter. We took our responsibility to hire just the right person very seriously. After all, our decision would impact the entire group, and we had been elected to the board to oversee the organization's business. We wanted someone with a work ethic we could approve of as well as someone who could relate to our members. With that in mind, we went into the interviews feeling the weight of responsibility."

The interview

"I was the second person interviewed. The candidate before me had been in the business for some time and already worked with a number of fishing groups. I know I can come across as a focused numbers guy, and fishing was a new industry for me, so I didn't think I stood a chance for the job - unless I could in some way stand out. Although what I said to make myself stand out was NOT something I anticipated saying.

Shortly into the interview, they asked me if I was bonded. And I replied, '*If you are asking whether I can be bonded, the answer is 'yes.' All of my arrests were based on circumstantial evidence.*' At first they all just stared at me, then one person laughed, and slowly each interviewer in turn 'got it.' That seemed to break the ice.

Although the rest of the questions were pretty standard, I think my impromptu joke made them see me as a person they could relate to. At least that was what I assumed when I got the job."

WINNING MOVES:

Since the interviewee is seldom privy to the specific history of the position they have applied for, or they make assumptions based on the few facts they do know, the perspective may not be the same for the interviewee as it is for the interviewers. That seems to be true in this instance. But sometimes the pieces magically fall together. And, as the board member who gave me the story for the context explained, it didn't hurt that the references for the successful candidate all emphasized his work ethic and integrity.

Unfortunately, the pieces do not always fall into place even if you do your homework. There is an element of unpredictability by the very nature of the activity. That's why interviews are stressful. But it also means that something unexpected can happen that will make things go *your* way. Like in this story.

Oh noooo!

"There is a reason there are books on first impressions; it doesn't take long to assess whether someone is going to be a good fit or not. And although when interviewing people you need to be consistent and jump through the same hoops with all candidates and toe the HR line, sometimes that can be very painful.

Most of our interviews for a technical trainer were running about an hour. We usually had about five team members and the HR person in the room for the interview. The HR person would provide an overview of the company and the position and then turn it over to the team to ask questions. We each had the same list of questions and took turns asking them. Then we would ask if the candidate had any questions. The final step was for the HR person to summarize next steps. A pretty standard, straightforward process.

We knew what we were looking for. We needed someone who could fit into a loud and fun-loving group, a person with lots of energy who could hold the attention of employees in a lengthy, detailed training session. Unfortunately, the instant this individual came into the room, we all knew she was not the right person. 'Drab' is the word that comes to mind – drab clothes, drab personality, monotonous voice - not only lackluster but completely lacking in anything resembling luster. But being conscious of the need for fairness, we started through our list of questions.

No matter how complex the question, her responses were brief and boring. It felt like she was slowly sucking all of the energy out of the room. It was all we could do to keep the interview going. In fact, I had to kick one of the interviewers to keep him from nodding off. But somehow we persevered, and after 25 minutes, we asked if she had any questions for us. She didn't. We were all starting to push our chairs away from the table to stand up when the HR representative said, 'Oh, if you don't have any more questions, I have a few I can ask.' She jumped right in before we could stop her.

The interview lasted the full hour. The longest hour in recorded history. Later we found out that the HR person felt sorry for the candidate and didn't want her to feel rejected. Although in the end, we had to do just that."

> **WINNING MOVES:**
> If you've ever had to go through a pile of resumes to identify viable candidates for a position, you know how difficult it can be to get a sense of the person from their professional credentials. Unfortunately, there can be a disconnect between what appears to be a qualified candidate on paper and the person who shows up for the interview. But then that's the reason for interviewing someone in the first place, isn't it? And no matter how cumbersome or frustrating the process is, consistency during the interview can help you avoid legal issues later on.

What are you looking for?

"I had recently turned an organization around and found myself in the enviable position of being recruited for a number of CEO openings in both small and large organizations. I soon discovered that there was a key question that told me what I needed to know about whether I wanted to be a part of the organization or not.

I made the discovery when I asked the board members of one organization what they were looking for in a CEO and got eleven different answers! They just couldn't agree. And based on his reaction to the question and responses, I got the distinct impression that their board chair wasn't looking for a CEO who would expect consistency and collaboration.

After several other lengthy interviews with different organizations, I had my shortest interview – about one and a half hours. The board members were very prepared and all in synch. This time when I asked what they were looking for in a CEO, I got consistent responses across the group. They wanted someone who cared about people, was tech savvy, and had worked in a variety of roles. There was no doubt in my mind that I was the person they were looking for."

WINNING MOVES:

Although it's easier to remember that the interview is a two-way street if you already have a job, it's important to go into the interview knowing what your ideal situation would look like. If you want to make sure the organization really *does* value its employees, for example, have a list of questions ready that will help you determine whether they do or whether they simply pay lip service to the concept. (What development opportunities are available? Are employees included in any bonuses for reaching business goals? What kind of communication exists between employees and executives? Etcetera). If you're clear in your mind about what you want, you will also probably be better at projecting the image that fits the criteria.

Management material

"When I first graduated from college I heard about an airlines job that put graduates in management positions simply because they were graduates. That sounded great to me. So I applied for a service representative position, fully anticipating that it was a stepping stone to management. During the interview I was asked where I saw myself in three-to five years and replied, with the confidence of someone who thought they knew how things worked in corporate America, that I expected to be in a management position in about six months and would probably go to graduate school in about three years.

Perhaps they weren't as familiar with their 'culture' as I was because I didn't get the job."

> **WINNING MOVES:**
>
> A person stops to ask directions in a small town and is told that her destination is "two see's" down the road. When she asks what that means, the response is: *"See that large tree on the horizon? Well, that's as far as you can see...so that's the first **see**. When you get there, you look as far as you can see, and that's the second **see**."*
>
> You can only see so far into the future; you can dream, but you still need to base each leg of your journey on what you can currently see.

Tell me about your family

"From the moment I walked in everyone was friendly and chatty. The interview itself was very informal. And, since I knew it was a small organization, I didn't hold them to the same HR standards I would expect of a larger organization. I willingly engaged in questions about family, children, and work habits. Then they asked me to sit in on, and participate in, one of their management meetings. It was an unusual interview tactic, but one that I enjoyed.

Although I was never certain the job was the best fit, I was pleased when they told me that I made the top three on their candidate list. Unfortunately – I think – they went with someone who had more relevant experience for their business. But I still remember the warmth and inclusiveness I felt during the interview process."

> **WINNING MOVES:**
>
> Although the organization crossed the line on what it is legal to ask during an interview, they demonstrated what a true "people focused culture" is like.

Chirping crickets

"I was flown in for a final interview for an HR Manager job for a large distribution warehouse with a HUGE retail company. The first part of the 'interview' was a tour of the area. The town isn't considered a hot spot for relocation, so the company wanted me to be sure I wanted to move there before they wasted more of their time and mine. Being driven around by the hiring manager for three hours was supposed to help me make the decision.

The intention was not to talk about the company or the work during the tour, but to get to know the town and for 'chit-chat.' Unfortunately, I am HORRIBLE at chit-chat, and the town didn't have much to offer for conversation starters. Not to mention, the hiring manager wasn't a particularly great conversationalist either.

About thirty minutes into the three-hour tour, I'd exhausted all of the non-personal questions and inquiries about the town and its people in my meager chit-chat repertoire. In the pauses that followed, one could hear the crickets chirping.

At one point I was really stretching for a conversation starter and said something completely ridiculous, so ridiculous that I've repressed the comment. But I remember that I turned my head away in shame as if I were an embarrassed teenager who had just said something incredibly stupid to a boy I had a crush on. I could feel myself wanting to mouth 'Oh My God.' I knew after that comment that I was sunk.

My recollection is that our 'tour' was cut a little short. I ended up in an office, alone, looking through some training manuals. The panel interview scheduled for the afternoon took all of about 30 minutes. I was asked to share only the worst elements of my past performance reviews, a question which took me by surprise. I've always had good performance reviews, and, in my mind, my answer ended up sounding arrogant and conceited.

The company didn't even call me to tell me I hadn't gotten the job - we all knew it when I left."

> **WINNING MOVES:**
> There are few things more discouraging than knowing you must continue, through to the end, an activity you know is futile.
> *"Courage doesn't always roar. Sometimes courage is the quiet voice at the end of the day saying, 'I will try again tomorrow.'"* Mary Anne Radmacher

Us and them

"The best question I've ever been asked in a job interview is: '*Of the four major racial groups, which do you get along with best and least well?*' My actual answer was far less astute than the one I should have given: '*Four? I thought there were just two - us and them.*'"

> **WINNING MOVES:**
> There are times when the questions you are asked in an interview tell you everything you need to know about what it would be like to work for a company. There's so much more to a job than a job description; use what you learn about the company during the interview to determine whether you really want the job or should run, not walk away. For example, one person told me about someone in her company who would always ask young women if they "had monthly mood swings." Apparently everyone just shook their heads over the fact that he was foolish enough to ask, and by some miracle, no applicant ever made an official complaint.

Conclusion:

Finding the right "fit" for a job where you spend so much of your time is an admirable goal. But it reminds me of the difference between crepes and pancakes – some things are just more complicated than others. Like culture. And like learning about an organization's culture during an interview. If fit is important to you, do your homework *before* the interview, including checking out blogs on the company. Then prepare a list of questions to ask. Find out how success is measured and rewarded, how promotions are made and whether people are promoted from within. Ask where HR falls in the hierarchy. Ask about employee development – who is developed and what kind of development opportunities are they given? In general, think about what is important to you, and get as many answers as you can before you have to make a decision. Use that three-way mirror to your advantage so you can see as much of their culture as possible in determining fit.

LESSONS LEARNED THE EASY WAY
(Through Someone Else's Experience)

Culture: Perceived culture fit can influence whether you get a job that you are otherwise qualified for. At the same time, you need to be tuned to the culture clues present during the interview to know whether you really want the job.

- *Know what to ask to get a picture of the organization's culture.*
  Determine what's important to you. Do you want a flexible schedule? Value personal development? Want to participate in cross-functional projects? Looking for advancement opportunities? Put together a list of questions to find out if what you want from the organization is something they are likely to support.

- *Make sure your personal values are consistent with the products and services of the company.*
  Companies want you to be engaged not only with the day-to-day function of your job but with their product and mission. It may seem obvious to say that the job and the company are part of the same package, but often times we focus more on the job than the company. Don't eliminate a job from consideration until after you've researched the company, but if you don't like what they do or stand for, it's wise to keep looking.

- *Don't assume that what happens in the interview is seen the same way by everyone.*
  We tend to think of an interview as an event that is anchored in an objective reality. But there are probably as many perspectives on what happened as there were people in the room. For example, you may feel like you knocked their socks off with an impressive presentation while they were thinking that someone with your set

of skills would be bored with the job in question. Also, there can be something that took place in the past that influences the hiring decision. There can even be an internal candidate that everyone is hoping to hire after they complete the legally required job search. The only thing you know for sure is whether you lived up to your own expectations.

- *Anticipate how you will respond if you are asked an illegal question or one that you don't want to answer.*
  Saying "you can't ask me that" to an interviewer will probably not endear you to the person. At the same time, you have to decide whether you will respond and how you feel about an organization that allows someone to ask an inappropriate question. In advance, think about what kinds of personal questions might come up and what you will say if they do. Keeping it light can get you through the interview. You can always decide afterwards if you want to say something more specific about the type of questions asked.

4

Boobs, Moth Holes, and Stray Hairs

The origin of "dressed to the nines" is generally thought to be unknown; but most consider the meaning to be a reference of scale. Assuming perfection is out of reach, nine would be the absolute best. The plural version - "nines" - is nothing more than people trying to make more of the number nine by fractionalizing it for further impact. In the past, being "dressed to the nines" for an interview meant a navy blue suit for women and a dark suit and conservative tie for men. But striving for perfection in dress looks different today than it did in the past. And the new dress code is not always clearly defined.

A recent article in *USA Today* spoke critically about job candidates wearing jeans, purple sweat suits, and spike heels or sneakers to interviews. They were also disapproving about how some applicants show up with pierced body parts and spiked hair. And they complained that others chewed gum or wore rumpled clothes or had their pants at half-mast. Their conclusion was that outlandish dress costs some candidates the job.

Once in the workplace, employees face possible restrictions on dress and appearance as well as negative reactions from other employees who may label cleavage, large or unusual tattoos and body piercing a major distraction. For example, according to a SHRM (Society for Human Resource Management) "Office Pulse" survey of more than 600 employees, 67 percent of those between ages 35-49 think tattoos in the workplace are okay, whereas 61 percent of those over 50 disagree and consider them not only inappropriate but distracting.

However, not all companies are the same in how they respond to popular trends. For instance, although many large companies have rules against visible tattoos and piercings, employees at Trader Joe's, Target and

Borders Books can be seen sporting tattoos and piercings. Similarly, Ford Motor Company allows all employees to have tattoos and piercings as long as there is no safety issue. Even Disney, known in the past for being conservative, has lifted its ban on employee goatees and other face fuzz. However, they do not permit tattoos, and employees who have them are allowed to use opaque makeup to conceal them, but not band aids.

Fashion faux pas for interviewing is definitely in the eye of the beholder, influenced by age, gender and profession. Do you wear fashionably tight pants or loose fit? Pantyhose or no pantyhose? Tie or no tie? (And, remember, according to tradition, if you wear a tie, it should lie over your belt buckle.) How many buttons on a suit do you fasten? Do you go out and buy something new or go with what's in your closet? The bottom line is, if you want the job, you may want to research the dress code before going in for the interview. Although given the stories that follow, that might not be enough.

Most of the following stories focus on how you determine what to wear to an interview, although several provide a somewhat different spin on the topic by bringing up some interesting questions, such as: Where do you change clothes for an interview no one at work knows you are going to? How do you cope with skirt creep? And can you tell from what the interviewer is wearing whether you will get the job or not? Most of us agonize over what to wear to an interview, but if these stories are any indication, it is hard to anticipate everything, even when it comes to dress.

Lights, camera, action

"My employer was unaware that I was applying for other jobs, so I didn't want to dress up for an interview I had that afternoon. I was planning on changing in the restroom and sneaking out the back door. But it was like my boss had a sixth sense about what I was planning to do. I couldn't seem to shake him. He was everywhere. So I never managed to change clothes while at work.

All the way to the interview I kept looking for places where I could stop and change clothes, but I didn't see any place that seemed appropriate. Finally I decided that I would park in their parking garage in a dark corner and change in the car. I found a spot that seemed okay and got into the back seat. It was harder than I thought it would be, especially since I had to take off slacks and put on nylons to wear with my suit skirt. But I managed it without working up too much of a sweat.

It wasn't until I got out of the car that I noticed the security camera…"

WINNING MOVES:

The moral to this story may be that the trend away from navy blue suits and nylons for women may make monitoring parking lot cameras less interesting. On the other hand, perhaps the lesson here is that the interviewee should consider modular clothing that can be dressed up or down by changing jackets and jewelry. Or, better yet, take a day off if you have an important interview that you are trying to keep secret.

Very, VERY informal

"Fortunately or unfortunately, I'm known as someone who is willing to listen to young people looking for jobs. So I get a lot of people coming to me for informational interviews. One young woman came to my office one day dressed inappropriately, what there was of it. She seemed smart, knew how to answer questions, and would have been a good candidate except for the fact that her dress definitely crossed a line. I decided to be honest with her.

CHARLOTTE L. STUART

'*You can never come to an interview dressed like you are,*' I said. '*You never know who you are going to be interviewing with. A female executive would have invited you to leave fifteen minutes ago. That blue suit that all of the books and articles talk about, that is never a bad choice.*'

She was surprised and thanked me for being candid with her. She said that she had heard that our organization was very informal, so she had felt comfortable wearing what she usually wore. Apparently 'informal' and 'scant' were synonymous in her vocabulary."

> **WINNING MOVES:**
> When it comes to dress for women in the workplace – especially for interviews – this poem says it all:
> *"Nothing too short.*
> *Nothing too bright.*
> *Nothing too low.*
> *And nothing too tight."*
> "Dress for Success" by Dr. Natasha Josefowitz

California casual

"My daughter was interviewing with a company that she was fairly familiar with, but just to be on the safe side, she asked about appropriate dress for the interview. She was told: 'professional business attire.' So she wore a jacket over a dress, casual yet professional from her point of view.

When she arrived she was greeted by a young woman wearing jeans, a flannel shirt, and a nose ring. Everyone else she met was similarly youthful and casually dressed. But she was still thinking that for a sales position being middle-aged and more professional looking might work in her favor.

During the interview she was asked how she felt about working there. She mentioned feeling overdressed but said that she assumed that for inter-

42

acting with clients that what she was wearing would be appropriate. They replied that their clients were 'casual.'

She wasn't surprised when she was told she was 'overqualified' for the job. That was obviously code for 'middle-aged and overdressed.'"

> **WINNING MOVES:**
> Sometimes it's difficult to define "casual." One of the stories I came across in an online blog was about a woman who came to an interview for a sales position wearing a painted-on denim jumpsuit and pink cowboy boots. I'm not sure if that was an instance of being over or under dressed. Perhaps it was an extreme example of California casual where "anything goes." Although having some taste in clothing never seems to go out of style.

Bashful bosom

"When I was younger I was tall and thin, but all of the women in my family are well-endowed. One summer during my college years, I had to swallow my pride and apply at a fast food chain restaurant, my first fast food experience. The interview with the young male manager was going well, until he started talking about uniforms. Turning his gaze to my chest, he began stroking his fashionable Miami Vice stubble and speculating.

'*Hmmmm, I think for your uniform we will need a size....well, let's see...I believe you might wear a size...*' With all of the pauses and thoughtful consideration, it felt like he had ogled my womanly form for several minutes by this point, but he finally withdrew his fascinated eyes from my bashful bosom and continued the interview.

Did I get the job? Do you really need to ask? However, to my everlasting relief, later that day I was offered another job at a different company. So I never had to venture into the world of fast food and even faster bosses."

WINNING MOVES:

Observation: breasts – covered and somewhat uncovered – can sometimes play an important role in the interview process. Although "we've come a long way, baby," in many ways there is still a long way to go.

Upward bound, in the material sense

"Although I never took the dress for success stuff too much to heart, I've always liked clothes. So when I had an important interview coming up, I went shopping. I bought an expensive and very nice suit that I felt made me look classy and professional. But of course that was when I was standing in front of the mirror in the dressing room.

When they invited me into the interview room and pointed to a chair, I didn't hesitate. It wasn't until I started to sit down that I realized that the shape of my skirt did not allow for modesty when in a seated position. As I sat, the skirt, that already had a short, fashionable slit in the side, slowly inched its way up my thighs. I pushed at it to no avail. The further down I went, the further up it went, and the more I was revealing. There was absolutely no question of crossing my legs!

I would like to think that the male interview panel chose me on my merits. But I never wore that suit again."

WINNING MOVES:

Fashion trends don't always work to the advantage of women. Years ago I asked a friend if she thought I could wear flats with a skirt for a consulting job interview. It was with a conservative bank where men in management were still required to wear white shirts and women didn't wear slacks. I still had a couple of skirts in my closet, but I had long since thrown out my high heels. Her response: "*Yes, but you won't get the job.*"

For the record, I wore flats and slacks to the interview and still got the job. And for the three months I was there I never met another woman wearing slacks. I got a lot of glares and stares, but no one admonished me for not complying with their dress code. But it could just as easily have gone the other way.

At a glance

"When the recruiter called me I was very excited. The position was with a small group in a large company, and the skill set needed could have been copied from my resume. I got past the initial interview with flying colors and looked forward to the next round. Since I knew the atmosphere at the company was fairly casual, I asked the recruiter about the appropriate dress for the interview. She told me that I should wear something I liked and felt comfortable in and that being formal was more negative than positive in their culture. That said, I spent more time fretting over what to wear than on what to say when I actually got there.

I was scheduled for three half hour interviews, one with each of the team members. I was feeling confident in my casual yet colorful jacket, dark slacks, and flat heeled walking shoes. Not quite business casual, more arty and outdoorsy than professional, the image I'd decided to project. The image I thought would make me instantly look like part of the team.

The first interview was with a young man who was wearing jeans and a T-shirt with something printed on it that I didn't quite get, but I wasn't comfortable asking what it meant. I wasn't even entirely sure I wanted to know, but it felt like a team test that I had flunked. We had an okay conversation, but he seemed relieved to pass me on to interviewer #2. This time I was with Rex Harrison from My Fair Lady. Formal attire, perfect diction, and posture any mother would have been proud of. He told me about what he was working on for a half hour. Then I was handed off to #3. The final tiny office was an amazing warren of piles of folders, books, and boxes. Everywhere you looked there were papers and stuff. And in the midst of the chaos sat the daintiest woman in a frilly, pink blouse, short skirt and very high heels. Her hair was perfect. Her make-up was perfect. She stared at me, and I stared at her. It should have ended there. Instead it ended a half-hour later."

> **WINNING MOVES:**
> We all know the power of first impressions. And we all know that the assumptions we make about people based on these first impressions can be way off. Nevertheless, in the interview process, you may not have enough time to get beyond them. Let's face it, how we dress DOES say a lot about how we view ourselves and how we want to be treated.

The moth hole advantage

"It was a job I really wanted. I liked everything about it. So by the time of the final interview, I was totally prepped for anything the hiring team could throw at me. And I knew my competition, so I was feeling confident. Not that he wasn't a viable candidate, but I was better.

When I didn't get the job, I swallowed my pride and asked for feedback. What I got surprised me. '*Well, it's hard to put into words,*' one of the interviewers who agreed to talk to me said. '*It's just that he was so…authentic. So real. He had a hole in the shoulder of his sweater…*' I didn't hear anything he said after that. Inside my head I was screaming *I could have worn something with a moth hole in it too!*"

> **WINNING MOVES:**
> Moth hole = authentic. I believe that there is something wrong with this cause and effect reasoning, although they may also have been correct in assuming that this individual cared more about the work than the impression he was making. But I bet the "hole in sweater" ploy wouldn't work twice!

Stray hairs

"I was excited about getting an interview with a large corporation for a really good job. On the day that I had an interview with three (female) peers and the VP, I wore my best suit and was really pumped. The interview with the peers went well until the very end. Since we just had a few minutes before the VP was scheduled to interview me, they wanted us to run to the restroom so they could 'tidy' me up. They told me that I had a few stray hairs and that wouldn't do. Also, did I have any makeup to freshen up my look? They explained that their VP was highly focused on details and that one of her favorite sayings was that she paid attention to the most minute of details 'down to the hair on a gnat.' (In order to tidy them up, no doubt.)

All three peers went with me to the restroom to help. While they made sure I looked appropriately tidy, they coached me on things to say and topics to avoid altogether. They probably thought they were helping me, but it was a bit much to take in at the last minute.

So, you may be wondering - did the VP have any stray hairs? Not a one. She was very pleasant, but she also appeared uptight, and, as warned, very detailed. Even her speech seemed measured, as though each word was carefully dusted off before being presented.

When I went home, I wrote my thank-you notes, and then withdrew myself as a candidate. The next day I deliberately left a few stray hairs dangling for effect. No one even looked twice."

> **WINNING MOVES:**
> Sometimes people *are* the stereotypes they appear to be. Read the signs.

Conclusion:

Dress codes are changing, but you need to know about expectations of the specific company you are interviewing with to be sure about what to wear. It depends on the type of company and its location. And even then, sometimes the expectations are different for an interview than for day-to-day work. Balancing self-expression with common sense may be a challenge at times. Showing respect by dressing up may be good advice in most instances, but there is always the exception. Researching the company and asking about dress codes should be part of the interview process. Still, "business casual" can mean different things to different people. And it can be different for men and women. In addition, some deviation from the organization norm may be acceptable if you are new to the workforce. It's a rapidly changing and unpredictable situation.

Perhaps the best online advice about dressing for an interview that I've come across is this: *Never wear uggs unless you want to let everyone know you have $150 to spend on boots and absolutely no taste.*

LESSONS LEARNED THE EASY WAY
(Through Someone Else's Experience)

Appearance: Knowing what to wear to an interview is more complicated than it used to be. What's acceptable for the workplace may still not be the right thing to wear for the interview.

- *Dress for an interview, not for a day at the office.*
  Most interviewers expect candidates to look their best for an interview. Not necessarily trendy or fashionable, but neat and professional. When dressing for the interview, ask yourself the following: 1) Is my outfit appropriate for the industry and for the position? 2) Does it show respect for the situation? 3) Does it show good judgment? If you can answer "yes" to these three questions, then you at least won't lose out on the job because of what you are wearing.

- *If you want to be casual but not too casual, wear something that you can modify when you arrive for the interview.*
  Have a jacket that you can remove. For women, a scarf or a piece of jewelry can add a bit of style and formality at the last minute. For men, it's a bit more straightforward. Simply wear a shirt that looks good without a jacket or tie.

- *For women, remember that cleavage and thighs are best kept out of sight.*
  The problem is that current fashion may be in conflict with what some people consider professional attire. In a day when female lawyers on television don't wear blouses under low-cut jackets, it may be hard to know what's acceptable. And young women in their twenties dress differently than older women. But you want those doing the interview to be looking you in the eyes and thinking about your answers.

- *Check with the company about their dress codes before the interview.* Dress codes usually include attitudes toward tattoos and body piercing as well as what is expected generally in terms of attire. Your image is a communications tool. If you want to make a statement by your appearance, be sure you can accept the consequences.

5
The Interview Milieu: Misery is Optional

Although the word milieu simply means the context or social setting within which something occurs, I not only love the way the word rolls off the tongue, but also the way it connotes an exotic backdrop for an event, a pervasive atmosphere of something larger than the surrounding geography. Consider the implications of the following usage examples for milieu:

> "*Theirs was a bohemian* **milieu** *in which people often played romantic musical chairs.*" —Edmund White, *New York Review of Books*, 12 February 2009
>
> "*This film is about a high-capitalist, haut-bourgeois* **milieu***, which is really anathema to me.*" —Tilda Swinton discussing her role in *I Am Love*, NPR online movie review, 4 July 2010
>
> "*The* **milieu** *of the crowds at the mall gave me such a headache.*" —answers.com.

A milieu is a complex mix of the social and the physical. It sets the scene for what takes place. But it may look different depending on your vantage point and the filter of expectations and hopes you bring to the table. That's why the title for this chapter includes the phrase "misery is optional."

In the following stories, the interview milieu runs the gamut: from a feeling of camaraderie due to a shared experience; to interview settings that create an almost other-worldly sense of time and place; to making a guess about expectations in a military setting. But in each instance, the milieu has an impact on the feelings and responses made by the interview participants.

Ticket to success

"I was on my way downtown to interview at a large organization for an accounting position. I'm not entirely sure why I was stopped and given a ticket. I may have misread a detour sign in an area where there was extensive construction going on. In any event, I accepted the ticket and proceeded to the interview. Not a particularly good start. Or so I thought–.

For some reason traffic tickets came up in the interview, and I mentioned what had happened to me on the way there. The interviewer confessed that he had received a ticket in that same spot, and we commiserated about being ticketed for something that didn't seem reasonable. We laughingly concluded that the city was trying to make some money by deliberately causing confusion in the construction zone.

The interviewer became my manager; the traffic ticket turned out to be my ticket to success."

> **WINNING MOVES:**
> In *What the Dog Saw*, Malcolm Gladwell uses a case study to look at the interview process. The object of this case study concludes that coming across as "confident in what you are doing and in who you are" is one of the key ingredients of a successful interview. This assumes you meet the minimum requirements for the job, of course. In the story about the traffic ticket, the act of sharing their common experience of being ticketed becomes the vehicle (pun intended) through which the two men are able to relax and be themselves. Thus, the interviewee assumes a confident, peer moment with his prospective boss.
> *"There is always one unexpected moment when the door opens and lets the future in."* Graham Greene

Written in the clouds

"I was working for a huge company that was very paternalistic and prided itself on hiring the top 10%. Since they already had the cream of the crop from their point of view, they liked to promote from within. That's why they asked me to set up an in-house interview training program that gave internal employees opportunities to practice their interviewing skills from the point of view of the interviewer and the interviewee.

I used managers to act as the interviewers to give them practice in a structured interview setting and thereby ensure that all candidates would be treated fairly. Participants in the workshop were video-taped so they would be able to see how they did and adjust accordingly when it was a real interview.

I particularly remember one young woman who interviewed in a room with a row of large windows. Every time she was asked a question she would turn to look out the window as if the answer was written in the clouds. They were good answers, but this nonverbal habit was very distracting.

When we reviewed the video, the potential candidate couldn't believe that she had actually looked out the window each time she answered a question. '*What was I doing looking out the window like that?*' she asked me. That was something I couldn't tell her. Nor did I have to give her the obvious feedback. On her own, she concluded, '*I'll have to work on that—*.'"

> **WINNING MOVES:**
> Sometimes the dominant feature of the milieu is the physical set-ting. But even that can have a huge impact on what happens in the interview. I'm surprised that more job applicants don't ask about the setting for the interview. As a speaker you always want to know what to expect. Room size, seating, presentation resources, light-ing, etc. Oh! I feel a story coming on...

One time I was asked to speak to a large audience, and the setting was a gymnasium. I wanted to test the acoustics and get a feel for what it would be like, so I made an appointment to check it out at a time when no one was around. I picked up the key at the main office and made my way to the gym. Getting inside was no problem but finding a light switch was. After searching for a while my eyes started adjusting to the dim light, so I decided not to walk all the way back to the office and embarrass myself by asking how to turn on the lights. Instead, I left the door propped open and made my way to the floor and started practicing my speech. Suddenly a dark figure in overalls appeared in the doorway. *"What the hell are you doing?!"* he yelled. Startled, I said the first thing that came to mind: *"Giving a speech."* *"Well, you need to keep the door shut,"* the voice yelled back as the door slammed closed. By the time I made it to the door in the dark, he was nowhere in sight. Later I found out that the lighting was controlled by a key operated wall switch.

I know you're there

"This happened to a friend of mine. It was an interview with the Federal government for an auditor position. When she arrived for the interview she was shown into a room and asked to sit at a specific table on the far end of the room away from the windows. The three interviewers then entered the room, introduced themselves and sat down at the table on the opposite end of the conference room with the window behind their backs. The effect was that my friend could not see the faces of the interviewers clearly. They had distinct forms, but were surrounded by light.

The three interviewers proceeded to move methodically through their list of questions, furiously scribbling notes on every response and providing no reaction or conversation. At the end of the interview, they thanked their candidate and ushered her out of the room without a clue as to how she had done. It was more like an interrogation by haloed saints than an interview.

The good news was that she was offered the job, and accepted."

WINNING MOVES:

What would YOU have done? Continued the interview without being able to see with whom you were speaking? Or would you have asked to change the setup? At least by calling attention to the issue you demonstrate that you are both aware of your surroundings and are comfortable enough to suggest alternatives. I once sat on a hump in the middle of a couch during an interview because I didn't want to appear to be picky about seating. Afterwards I realized that all I had to do was move over; I didn't even need to say anything. And, if someone had asked, I could have told the truth – it was very uncomfortable sitting on a big bump.

Some people assume that the interview milieu is a reflection of the company culture. If so, the set-up in this story suggests that either the interviewers were insensitive to the candidate's comfort or were oblivious to the situation. If the latter, then they can perhaps be forgiven. And if the candidate had mentioned the problem, they would most likely have been quick to make accommodations. But if the set-up was the result of insensitivity, either before or after noticing what was happening, then that doesn't speak highly of the individuals involved and the culture within which they operate. Since she accepted the job, let's hope it was the former.

Be my guest

"Years ago I spent a year studying abroad in Germany. At the end of my studies I didn't want to leave. But in order to stay longer I needed to get a job. The only way that seemed possible was if I got one on a military base.

The day of my interview I found the right building and the right floor, but the room was in a chained off area. I wasn't sure if I should go in or not on my own, but decided I had no choice.

I had just removed the chain and stepped through when I saw this guy watching me. Time froze as we made eye contact. He looked aggressive, and I figured he knew I wasn't supposed to be doing what I was doing. Hoping that politeness would win out over an alpha male challenge, I pulled the chain back, stepped aside and let him walk through.

Politeness *did* pay off when five minutes later I was sitting across from him for my interview. I got the job."

> **WINNING MOVES:**
> Some organizations operate under a formal hierarchy, and it's likely that's true of employees on a military base. But as an outsider it may be difficult to know exactly what is expected of you. In this instance, the individual apparently made the right choice. Although being polite usually goes a long way in any situation. For example, I've heard several stories about interviewees who did not show sufficient respect to the administrative assistant while waiting to be interviewed. Afterwards they were surprised to find out that the admin had made their rudeness known to the decision makers.

Queen for an hour

"They started with 86 candidates and got it down to 5 all in the same day! Then the approximately 20 stakeholders interviewed the 5 remaining candidates. I was one of those. They sat on either side of a long table with me seated at the narrow space at the front. Slowly they went around the room and asked their assigned question. I felt like I was holding court, dispensing wisdom from my office chair throne."

> **WINNING MOVES:**
> Many organizations use this format, and it can be intimidating. One piece of advice is to be careful not to focus just on the person asking the question when responding, but try to include everyone in your response. And in spite of the intimidation factor, do not hesitate to ask for clarification if you don't get the point of the question.

French court

"Picture a large board room. A sense of space and elegance. High-backed chairs. A long polished wood table. Three interviewers seated on one side. Me on the other.

I can still imagine myself in that moment in space and time, the sense of ritual and formality. Like being in front of the three judges in a French court! Even some of the questions had a judicial tone. One that I remember was: 'If we walked around department X, what would we hear people saying about you?'

That I'm not guilty..."

> **WINNING MOVES:**
> Again, the milieu is both the feel and the context. And it may or may not reflect some critical piece of the organizational structure and culture. You need more information in order to be certain.

Ten dollars a day

"I knew I wouldn't get the job even before I went to the interview. I was trying to move from being an assistant editor to being a full editor, but in a conversation on the telephone with the director, it had already been determined that I didn't have enough experience for what he needed. Despite that, I set up an informational interview with him, figuring that at least I could make a new contact in the industry. I felt quite proud of myself. I mean, isn't that what you're supposed to do?

The day of the interview, I made sure to catch the subway a bit early, so that I wouldn't be late. This was before GPS and his place was in a part of town I didn't know very well. When I arrived, I rang his bell right on the dot, but nothing happened. Nothing. I pulled my calendar out of my bag and verified that I was at the right door at the right time. Then I buzzed a couple more times. Finally, a rather sleepy voice came out over the intercom. After a bit of confusion, a longer explanation, and some strange looks from passersby, I was buzzed in.

It was clear that I'd woken him up. He explained that he needed to take a shower because he had an appointment. Then he set me up in his living room to watch some footage from his upcoming film. I could hear the shower water running in the background. He came back, thankfully dressed, and explained that he was off to visit an old synagogue in the Lower East Side of New York which he was hoping to rent out for a fundraiser. Did I want to come, he asked. Sure, I said. I figured it was the only way I was going to get a chance to talk to him and, heck, I'd always wanted to see the inside of one of those old buildings.

We chatted a bit, got a nice tour of the synagogue, and by the time we were walking back, the conversation had begun to take on a nice flow. He was complaining about how difficult it was to find good interns. By the time you found one, broke them in, and showed them the ropes, they tended to take off. *'I can't seem to keep an intern for more than six months!'* he said. Trying not to balk at this comment, I told him about my first film internship experience where I had only earned ten dollars a day. That had made it hard to stick around for very long. Yes, he agreed. At his first internship, he had only made a hundred dollars a week! I decided not to mention that one hundred dollars a week was twice ten dollars a day.

I never regretted not getting that job, although his film did quite well."

WINNING MOVES:

This story illustrates that you never know what to expect when you go for an interview. Prepare, but be prepared to be surprised.

Conclusion:

No matter what happens during the interview, two things are true. First, you come away with a story, and second, "misery is optional."

LESSONS LEARNED THE EASY WAY
(Through Someone Else's Experience)

Environment: The interview milieu – context or social setting – within which the interview takes place can help or hinder the candidate. The key is to quickly assess the milieu and decide what you can do to either improve the situation or adapt to it.

- *"Never let them see you sweat."*
  The above phrase is code for displaying confidence no matter how you feel inside. Most interviewers want to see a display of composure and self-assurance. By displaying the self-confidence to adapt to an awkward situation or by requesting a change in your surroundings, you send the message that you are comfortable with yourself and others.

- *If the opportunity arises, don't hesitate to talk about a common experience or interest that you share with an interviewer. But keep it brief.*
  In the first story in this chapter, two men bond over a traffic ticket. Don't be afraid to go off script, but stay alert to nonverbal cues as to how the conversation is being received. There is a fine balance between being too chatty and seeming aloof.

- *Always be polite.*
  This was good advice when your mother gave it to you, and it's still good advice. Being polite keeps your options open.

- *Try to find out whether there is a link between the interview milieu and the organization's culture.*
  Just because the interview setting is formal doesn't mean the organization's culture is characterized by formality. But it suggests some questions you might want to ask. For example, who is included

in planning sessions? Does the CEO communicate directly with employees? What avenues are there for submitting suggestions? Or, if you are subjected to multiple interviews with different groups, you might want to ask questions about attitudes toward collaboration, accountability standards, or whether there are merit raises or bonuses based on performance, etcetera. The milieu may or may not reflect the culture, but you won't know unless you ask the right questions.

- *Ask about the interview setting in advance.*
  If your contact person doesn't tell you how many people will be interviewing you or how long the interview is expected to last, ask. Also, ask whether there is anything you should bring to the interview or anything you can do to prepare. That said, don't feel betrayed if what actually happens isn't what you were told. Go with the flow.

6

Honesty and Other Disasters

"Tell me I'm clever, Tell me I'm kind, Tell me I'm talented, Tell me I'm cute, Tell me I'm sensitive, Graceful and wise, Tell me I'm perfect – But tell me the truth."

Poem by Shel Silverstein

We all know that the "unvarnished truth" does not always go over well. Yet culturally we seem to have bought into the philosophy that honesty is the best policy. We tend to deride the "spin" that some politicians and news agencies put on the facts. And in the workplace we talk a lot about trust, open communication, walking the talk, and the need for transparency. At the same time we also praise tact, diplomacy, and discretion. We understand that facts can be misleading. And we are constantly packaging and repackaging ourselves for professional networking and the social media. It's no wonder that the line between truth and image can become blurred.

So what are the parameters of honesty in the interview setting? Is putting your best foot forward slightly dishonest? What about the omission of some of your bad decisions or project failures? Are you obligated to confess "real" faults and shortcomings when asked about your weaknesses? Unfortunately, telling it like it is may not help you land the job you want, but where do you draw the line and still maintain credibility as an honest person?

In this chapter you will find tales of both honesty and dishonesty. Not surprisingly, the stories about flagrant dishonesty are told from the perspective of the interviewer, not the interviewee. No one apparently wanted to brag about being dishonest. Although there is one story about "packaging" that could be categorized in the dishonest column and is told by the person it happened to. And, as you might expect, in most but not all of the stories about dishonesty, the people who lied paid a price for lying. But if the stories about honesty are any indication of the norm, then being honest doesn't necessarily give the candidate an edge either. There can apparently be too much truth telling during an interview, or the truth may be delivered in an unpalatable way.

Playing the Odds

"I, as a freshly minted attorney (one who recently passed the bar), was given a job interview by an established law firm in Carson City, NV. Eager to explore this opportunity to move from a major metropolitan area and begin my legal career in this small city near picturesque Lake Tahoe, I drove several hundred miles to be interviewed.

As requested by the firm, I met the firm's partners for lunch at a restaurant located in a prominent Carson City casino. At one point in the lunchtime conversation, the partners informed me that their principal client was the very casino in which we were having lunch. They asked me if I would have any problem with becoming a legal advocate for a gambling casino. In an attempt to provide an answer that would not only appear positive to the partners but also be an honest expression of my own good character, I spoke confidently. I told them I would not have a problem representing a casino if it fully informed the gamblers of the odds against them winning, such as by posting a conspicuous notice at each game site stating the odds relating to that game.

The conversation stopped momentarily until one of the partners emphasized, in a sort of you-do-understand-don't-you tone that suggesting such an odds-notification (which apparently was not a legal requirement at the time) would probably be frowned upon by the firm's casino clients. Soon thereafter, the meeting was concluded, without any further reference to the firm's casino clients. I was not offered the job."

> **WINNING MOVES:**
> Two quotations capture the conundrum presented by this interview situation.
> *"To be direct and honest is not safe."* William Shakespeare, *Othello*
> Put somewhat differently:
> *"No one wants the truth if it is inconvenient."* Arthur Miller

Checkered past

"I was just finishing up my undergrad work and had applied to Duke University for graduate school. Since most of my final exams came at the end of the exam period, I decided to take a little vacation. The little vacation turned out to be quite a good time, and I didn't make it back to take my exams. That resulted in four 'ABs' on my transcript (absent from exam). I was able to make up the exams, but not before my interview for grad school.

My interview was with THE important person in my area, a no bullshit guy who was pretty intimidating. I wasn't quite sure how to respond when he said, *'I've never seen a resume like this before; this is spectacular. I assume these ABs are A+, right?'*

It was tempting, but either way it was a risk. *'It means I was absent from the exams,'* I confessed.

'What were you doing?' he asked.

I couldn't think of anything to say other than the truth. *'Basically, I was partying at the beach.'*

He thought for a moment, then said, *'I've never had someone tell me a story like that. You are in.'* I wasn't sure if it was because of my honesty or if he, too, liked a good party."

> **WINNING MOVES:**
> Okay, so the unvarnished truth can sometimes work to your advantage. But based on the outcome of the previous story, you can't assume truth is always the best policy – not if you want the job. On the other hand, if you lie, punishment may just be delayed. My advice is to combine diplomacy with truth. As long as you don't cross any legal or ethical lines.

The dog ate it

"It was my first HR position, and one of my tasks was to do resume checks. Because of a large government contract we received, we had to verify the credentials of all of the supervisors overseeing the project. As it turned out there was a problem with one of the supervisors who had been with the company for a time. He didn't have a copy of his transcript, and I couldn't verify his educational credentials. The school he said he had attended in Canada had burned down, and all of their records along with it. It was like the homework the dog supposedly ate.

When I asked my boss what I should do, he said to set up a meeting with the supervisor. During the meeting it didn't take long for my boss, skilled in interview techniques, to elicit a confession. Apparently, the supervisor had been losing out to younger, less experienced people with degrees and decided to 'get' one for himself. He was mortified to be found out, but my boss was intrigued. He wanted to know how the man had located possibly the only university in the Americas that didn't have any records. He was so impressed by the feat that he was willing to give the guy a second chance…IF his references checked out. They were all spot on, and he continued to be an excellent employee, although he wasn't able to be a supervisor on the new project. And he had to fill out a new application."

WINNING MOVES:

The popular story about George Washington confessing to cutting down the cherry tree and thus displaying his honesty may have inspired this employee. Or maybe he simply felt trapped into telling the truth. In either case, he was fortunate that the individual making the decision was willing to bend the rules for an otherwise exemplary employee. Most employees caught in this kind of lie are ushered out the door post-haste.

Too much sharing

"I worked for state government for a very long time. Years ago, I interviewed a man who was very qualified, had worked for other government offices, and actually interviewed quite well. Towards the end of the interview, he said, '*I should probably tell you because you are going to find out anyway. I am a convicted felon.*' I said all of the appropriate legal speak…being a felon doesn't necessarily prevent you from working here, etc. And I meant it.

He then pulled out a copy of a newspaper article that talked about how he was arrested and convicted for stealing money from the last government agency he worked for. A simple statement of fact was one thing, but sharing the newspaper coverage with me seemed a bit strange. Needless to say, that concluded the interview and he didn't get the job. The irony is that I probably would not have found out since the agency he stole from was in another state, and, at the time, our state only ran background checks on our own state's convictions."

WINNING MOVES:

The candidate should probably have confessed that he chopped down a cherry tree instead of proving beyond a doubt that he stole money from a government agency!

Appearances can be everything

"We were looking for an executive with a solid public affairs background and were pleased to find someone who seemed to have both the education – an MA in Public Affairs from a good university – and the right amount of experience. We brought him in for an interview. He had some very convincing stories of great successes. He appeared to be personable, intelligent, and a good fit for the organization. And his references were stellar. So we hired him.

There is always a settling in period, so it took us a while to realize that everything he presented at meetings came from his staff, not from him. He was outstanding at regurgitating information in reports and presentations, although his presentation style was rather robotic. And he sometimes had difficulty answering questions about the material.

When staff members complained that he really didn't know what he was doing, we dug deeper into his resume and discovered that his MA was nonexistent, his degree was in art history, and he had never even taken a single class in public affairs! Appearances can be everything, but they can also be deceiving."

> **WINNING MOVES:**
> It makes you wonder what his references said about him, doesn't it? Did the person calling his references think it was strange that he received kudos for his groundbreaking article on the iconography in the works of Mark Podwal? The bottom line: lying on your resume is never a good idea.

Falsification foible

"You may not remember all of the projects you've worked on, or all of the people you've worked with, but there are some projects and some people that stand out for one reason or another. In one interview, both a project and a person from the past came together in a unique and memorable way.

I was leading an interview panel. One of the interviewees turned out to be someone I had supervised several years earlier. She had been a part of a team working to resolve a complicated technical problem.

Imagine my surprise when, during the interview, she touted as one of her major accomplishments being the lead of the team that had resolved this major technical problem. Could this be true, I wondered? Did she just claim to have been *my* supervisor? Yes. Hutzpah? Yes.

Did she get the job? No."

WINNING MOVES:
Research shows that some people have difficulty with facial recognition, but that's no excuse for the above mistake. If there is anything worse than lying on your resume, it's lying about your accomplishments in front of someone who knows the truth.
Advice? Don't do it.

Shotgun interview

"I was interviewing a candidate who was well qualified for the position, but he had been in the same job for a long time, so I was curious what was prompting him to finally change roles. When I asked why he applied for the position, he replied that his wife felt he needed a better job!

Although I appreciated his honesty, I was shocked by the admission. It felt like a shotgun interview, not the result of someone who really wanted to commit to the job."

WINNING MOVES:
Maybe he should have interviewed the candidate's wife.

It doesn't "speak to me"

"The recruiter talked real fast and was very abrupt. So when she asked me why I wanted to work for the company, I gave a pretty succinct but honest response. I told her that I only knew what I had researched and read on their website and that one of the things I would want to do is to find out more about their business and culture. Then she asked me if I had watched the recruiting video.

Well, I had. It involved some lovely scenes of a nearby city before mentioning that the actual location was 20 miles away. Then a drab building came into view and a young man jumped out from the side and announced that he was the 'coffee man' and that he just loved the people who worked there. Finally, they went inside and moved from cubicle to cubicle with people drably saying that they 'loved' the company. The clip ended with tightly edited faces of people perkily saying 'Creative!' 'Friendly.' 'Rewarding!'

Since I couldn't tell her too directly that the recruiting video was a turn-off rather than a selling point, I simply said that it didn't 'speak to me.' She responded by letting me know that other people really liked it."

WINNING MOVES:

Unfortunately, it can be difficult to gauge when someone will have a proprietary feeling about something. It's like being shown a picture of someone's new baby. Although in that instance you know what you *should* say even if you think the baby is unattractive and doesn't resemble the parents in any obvious way. But when it's a marketing piece, you might think there is room for a difference of opinion as to its effectiveness. Obviously in this case, there wasn't. Some companies consider it an act of disloyalty to question anything related to their brand. It's hard to know whether the interviewer's response was indicative of the culture or just this one person. It's gray areas like this that make the interview process both challenging and unpredictable.

When "we" should be "me"

"Corporate America makes a big thing out of teamwork and being a team player. So it was easy to fall into the trap of emphasizing my work as part of a team effort and forget to promote myself. I realized too late that I left the impression that I was unable to achieve results on my own. Needless to say, I didn't get the job. Ironically, I'm often the person on the team who makes sure things get done. As the saying goes, 'there may not be an 'I' in teamwork, but there's an 'm' and an 'e.'"

> **WINNING MOVES:**
> Honesty, self-promotion, and cultural influences collide in this story. Corporate America loves a team player, but they also love a leader. Managing that balance in describing your skills can be a challenge during an interview.

Sports fan

"Although I've never been a sports fan, I was impressed by a quotation from a famous football player and used it as a theme for my cover letter for a job with a telecommunications company. It was just a way to get my foot in the door; I never expected it to become an issue during my interview.

When I arrived for my interview, the television was on and several people were gathered around watching a football game, obviously very involved in who was winning and losing. One of the watchers turned out to be the VP I was scheduled to meet with. On the way into his office, with him looking back over his shoulder at the television, he asked who I was rooting for. I said, '*Oh, I'm not much of a sports fan.*' *That* got his attention.

There was a folder with my name on it on his desk. He flipped it open and scanned the page on top. Then he looked at me and asked why I had used the quotation I had to talk about my values and approach to work. It didn't seem like a good idea to say I thought *he* would relate to it. Nor could I say much about the individual I had quoted – because I didn't know anything about him other than what I had quoted. It quickly became clear that what I had written was a gimmick and not sincere. In the end, I was not destined to participate in their football pool."

> **WINNING MOVES:**
> Marketing your skills requires creativity. With so many people out there applying for jobs, it can be difficult to grab a recruiter's attention. Obviously the advice given to writers in general applies here – write about something you know about. Or else start reading the sports page.

May I be bluntly frank? Or frankly blunt?

"They initiated a Voluntary Personal Protection program at work. They then gave you handbooks with activities, and you had to fill out 'passports' logging the activities. Granted the goals of the program were good, especially in an industry where there are a lot of safety issues, but to me, the key word was 'voluntary.'

When I was approached to interview for an internal position, I decided to go through the process, although I wasn't sure I wanted the job. There were two interviewers. I knew one of them, an Eagle Scout who thought it was more important to sing Happy Birthday to employees than to make sure they had the proper tools to do their jobs. But a good guy nonetheless. The second interviewer was the supervisor for the position. I had been warned by several people, even one who didn't much care for me, that this woman and I were not a good fit.

The first part of the interview was pretty straightforward. 'Tell us a little about yourself,' that sort of thing. Then I was asked (by the Eagle Scout) whether I had completed my VPP (Voluntary Personal Protection) Passport. I said that I was curious why he had asked me that question since the program was voluntary and therefore inappropriate to bring up in an interview.

Then the other interviewer presented me with a scenario: what would I do if a supervisor or mechanic I'd been in conflict with in the past refused to let me perform my auditor role? I explained that I would first talk with them and try to work it out. If that failed, I would have my supervisor make arrangements for another auditor to do the job.

The interviewer did not like my response. She said, *'But if that IS your assignment, you're supposed to figure out how to do it.'*

I explained that it was my opinion that you should not stop a job because of personality conflicts. The only two reasons for a stop was injury to personnel or damage to equipment. I added that if that was their way of thinking, then I was probably not the person for the job. Because that way of doing things created foes and not partners. She agreed with the former but not the latter: I was not the right person for the job.

At a later date, I was given some excellent advice by someone who felt I had a lot of potential. He told me that there is a difference between speaking frankly and speaking bluntly. The goal is to frame your argument so you can get along with anyone. But that doesn't mean you would want to work for someone who constantly challenged that principle."

WINNING MOVES:

"Tell me the truth, how did you think my presentation went?" I've been asked this type of question many times by colleagues. The desire to be kind is often in conflict with the urge to give constructive feedback. As a former speech coach, I can't listen without thinking about ways to improve a presentation. It's in my DNA. I have learned, however, that even sincere requests for feedback require sensitivity to timing and language. Whether framing an argument or giving feedback, there is more at stake than simply being bluntly honest.

Trial run

"I had been employed at the same job for far too long and was looking for a change. So I definitely wasn't interested in applying for a position in the same industry I was trying to leave. But my wife convinced me that it would be good to practice my interviewing skills. Then when the right job came along, I would be better prepared.

I went into the interview totally relaxed. I didn't care what happened, so I could enjoy myself. I was able to be open, honest, direct, transparent – saying exactly what I wanted to say whether I thought it was what the interviewer wanted to hear or not. We had a lively discussion, disagreeing on some things, on the same page on others. It was comfortable, engaging, and animated.

What can I say – we bonded. He liked my straightforward approach to work and the business, and I liked him. I ended up being offered and accepting the job."

> **WINNING MOVES:**
> This is how every interview should go. An open exchange of ideas in a relaxed atmosphere. Unfortunately, most of us find that "being ourselves" in a stressful situation is difficult to achieve. The best we can sometimes hope for is a near facsimile.

Conclusion:

An example used to explain the concept of framing has stuck with me. It was an experiment to find the "best" way to present the odds for a particular surgical procedure. In one instance patients were told: *Out of 100 surgeries, 10 people die.* Another group was told: *Out of 100 surgeries, 90 survive.* More people opted for the surgery when they were told the latter. Some might argue that this is manipulative or that increasing the number who opt for the surgery is not the best outcome. But the point is that by changing how you present facts, you influence how they are received.

Honesty is not a straightforward concept. It can take many forms without moving into the realm of dishonesty. And even if you accept the premise that honesty is the best policy, no matter how you frame it, there are consequences.

LESSONS LEARNED THE EASY WAY
(Through Someone Else's Experience)

Honesty: Honesty, particularly in the context of an interview, is not a straightforward concept. For example, is putting your best foot forward compatible with being completely honest? And how much transparency is necessary when asked about your weaknesses?

- *Know the difference between diplomacy and the unvarnished truth.*
  Some questions require a yes-no response, but most give you latitude to explain your answer. You can disagree by saying, "I see this issue from a different perspective…" But, it is usually better to ask a clarifying question rather than making a statement. "Let me make sure I understand what you are asking…" That gives you time to think, and possibly find common ground.

- *Never lie on your resume.*
  There are too many ways to get caught if you lie about your credentials or experience. Some people are really good at puffing up the facts; but many hiring managers are just as skilled at deflating them.

- *Research the individuals who will be interviewing you.*
  They know about you; it's only fair that you know something about them. What degrees do they hold? Where have they worked? Who do they know that you might know? Audience adaptation is not dishonest, it's a skill.

- *Know when to cut your losses.*
  Know what kind of environment you would like to work in and ask questions to determine fit *before* you accept an offer. For example, if you want to know whether the culture values politeness over straightforward feedback, ask questions about decision making and

process improvement. If you like a little competition, ask about the reward system and opportunities to excel. Even if you don't know what kind of environment you prefer, by asking questions like these, you will be better prepared for success if you are offered and accept the position.

7
Didn't See That Coming

Everyone agrees that you need to prepare carefully for an interview – learn everything you can about the company and position, practice responses to potential questions, and make lists of questions you want to ask them. In fact, people writing about the interview process usually advise that it never hurts to over-prepare. But no matter how much time and effort you put into the preparation phase, there is always the possibility that something unexpected will occur. And even if things go as you anticipated, you could still go off script or say something off the top of your head that surprises even you.

After an interview it's not uncommon to relive the entire session, thinking of what you could have said to wow the interviewers. Or wishing that you hadn't said something that you are certain has ruined your chance to land the job.

> *"All the Woulda-Coulda-Shouldas*
> *Layin' in the sun,*
> *Talkin' bout the things*
> *They woulda-coulda-shoulda done...*
> *But those Woulda-Coulda-Shouldas*
> *All ran away and hid*
> *From one little did."*
>
> Poem by Shel Silverstein

Most of the stories in this chapter are about people who felt like they *should* have anticipated what happened and were mad at themselves for not doing so. But several of the stories have happy endings. One because of something positive that the person didn't anticipate, another because of something funny that happened that they didn't anticipate, and a third where anticipating a potential obstacle definitely paid off. Even if there are no guarantees, playing the "what if" game *before* the interview can make you more resilient *during* the interview.

Telltale pause

"Several years after taking early retirement from a corporate law department and establishing my own solo law practice, I contemplated going back to work at another corporation. I was invited to meet a manager and his superior, a director, who had management authority over the position I was seeking. Those meetings went well and about a week later I was invited back to meet some other personnel and the vice president in charge of the group.

After talking with these additional people, the manager walked with me through the facility's 'campus' to the parking lot. During the walk, the manager (who had confessed that he was looking forward to his own retirement) asked if I was really sure I wanted to give up my autonomy. The question caught me a bit off guard, causing me to pause, to think of what the question implied about the prospective work environment, and to conclude that I was not sure.

I attempted to provide a reasonably truthful, although ambiguous response by assuring the manager that of course I enjoyed my autonomy, but I also liked working with others in a good organization. Perhaps the pause was a 'tell.' I was not invited back a third time."

WINNING MOVES:

We all have blind spots. After the fact you may feel like you should have anticipated a particular question. One of the hardest things to do is to forgive yourself for tripping up over something that "shoulda" been an easy win.

Interview 101

"There are some interview 101 questions that you can anticipate. Especially if you know that the interviewer personally knows someone you work with. Especially when that someone is a person who pops into your head the instant you are asked to describe a work issue that you have found challenging!

That's what happened to me. So when I found myself talking off the top of my head about my challenges with her rather than giving a wise and insightful response, I was not pleased with myself. Although I wasn't terribly disappointed, because the job wouldn't have been a good fit for many reasons, it was an interview mistake that I won't make again."

> **WINNING MOVES:**
> Another "shoulda." And a lesson learned.

Please make it stop

"I was pleased to be referred for a job at a large U.S. conglomerate and receive an email to have an initial discussion with the hiring manager. At the appointed time on a Monday morning, the phone rang. As I picked it up I was pretty sure that like many other initial discussions this would be more focused on the interviewer explaining about the position vs. actually interviewing me. But it wasn't.

From the first moment the interviewer honed right in on my education and then went chronologically through my resume, wanting me to walk through experiences which had become dim and distant memories. As the conversation proceeded I began to feel more and more as if my mouth was filled with cotton wool! My answers become more and more fuzzy and disconnected. It was pure torture.

We had allocated 1 hour for the interview, but by 45 minutes in I was praying for the tables to be turned, anticipating the opportunity to stop waffling about my experience and ask him some questions. No such luck.

For a very long 1 hour and 15 minutes I endured a grilling. When he finally asked, '*Is there anything you'd like to ask me about the position?*' I knew it was too late to save the interview. It was a humbling experience and a great lesson!"

WINNING MOVES:

If you have gone through the interview process a number of times, you start to expect a certain formulaic sequence of events. But sometimes the person on the other end of the line or across the table from you doesn't stick to the script. Instead of taking a Zen moment to regroup, it's probably more likely that you will experience a panic attack. Expect the unexpected, and when it happens, either adapt to the new approach or see if you can buy yourself some time to think. For example, you might ask about the process.

"I assume by the way you've started our conversation that you intend to focus our discussion on my resume – is that correct?"

If the answer is "yes," then see if you can minimize the time spent doing that by attempting to drive the conversation in a slightly different direction. You might mention that you have a few questions about the position or the company and ask it would be okay to address those before continuing with the resume discussion. Or, maybe you can turn the tables slightly by asking how something on your resume relates to how this particular company does things.

"Yes, I've had experience with global projects – I'm curious what kind of large, international projects Company X is involved with."

Obviously, you shouldn't sound like you are trying to deflect a discussion about your resume particulars, but broadening the conversation may be not only acceptable but an indication that you are relating your experience to the job in question. If you feel backed into a corner, it's definitely worth a try.

No questions, thank you

"I grew up in a culture where women didn't ask questions; rather, they responded when spoken to. They were supposed to be demure, soft-spoken, and good listeners. Not all of that rubbed off on me, but enough of it did that it had an impact on my first interview after college.

I went prepared to answer questions…and that's what I did. I spoke when spoken to, in a voice that I felt was appropriately modulated but which might have been interpreted as unenthusiastic or timid. Although I didn't realize that at the time. Then, when they reached the end of their questions, they asked if I had any. 'No,' I said.

That was the end of the interview and my chance for the position.

It's been years since that happened, and I now know what I'm supposed to do to be perceived as a forceful and competent manager. But there are times when I think it would be easier to wear a button proclaiming my internal, dynamic personality rather than trying to behave that way."

WINNING MOVES:

"Be yourself" isn't always the best advice. And who you are today is not who you will be tomorrow. We all learn and grow. At the same time, there may be personality characteristics that are an integral part of who we are. We can adapt ourselves and our behaviors to succeed at a particular job, but there may also be instances when the stretch isn't worth it in the long run. We need to make conscious decisions about fit and growth if we are to be happy in the workplace.

Two in one

"When I was interviewing candidates for an outreach and development position, it soon became clear that there were 'outreach' types and 'development' types, and no one seemed to be both. The development people were internal, fact oriented, and computer literate. They tended to be reserved. Precise. Well organized. Competent. But people I couldn't picture impressing reporters or creating innovative themes for an outreach campaign. On the other hand, the outreach candidates were open, friendly, social, talkative. Again, very professional, but in a different way. It was difficult to image them tied to a desk for any length of time, and there was a lot of organization and computer time required for the position.

The differences between the two types also revealed themselves by their choice of interview follow-up. Which do you think sent the 'Dear Mr. ____' email versus the musical thank-you card?

I had just about decided that I would have to choose between the two positions when someone applied who seemed to have both sets of qualities and experience. I was leery but hopeful when I asked him to come in for an interview.

It was easy to spot the charm right away. The pleasant smile, easy chit-chat, comfortable demeanor. For the other qualities I had to rely on his resume and my very clever behavioral interview questions. But in the end, I hired him, half expecting a Doctor Jekyll and Mr. Hyde transformation when he stayed in the office versus when he went out to meet people. But it was soon clear that he was truly a 'two in one' individual, equally adept at both roles."

WINNING MOVES:

People are drawn to certain professions for a variety of reasons — pay, aptitude, experience, image, opportunity. Some find their niche early on and focus their professional lives in a narrow way. Others may not only be capable of doing a number of things well but enjoy the variety. Sometimes jobs and job categories change, and people are forced to make new decisions about how to earn a living. I once asked someone how he became a commercial fisherman, and he told me it was because his job as a boilermaker went away. And he knew someone who was a commercial fisherman. For him it turned out to be an easy transition. Unfortunately, that's not always the case. But, as George Eliot said, *"It is never too late to be what you might have been."*

Shoulda said "no"

"I had just started my consulting business and went to pitch myself for a project that didn't look that appealing – but I wanted the work, so I didn't want to say 'no.' It wasn't as much a training job as being the person to present some unpleasant changes in policy that the company's management didn't want to communicate themselves.

The third party who had been given the task of finding a 'trainer' spoke with me first. Then she left me to look at the perfectly horrible 'training materials.' Next she took me in to talk to the internal head of HR. He spoke to me for all of two minutes, asked to excuse himself, motioning to the third party headhunter to come outside with him. She returned less than a minute later, said I wasn't a good fit, and that was that.

Why is it you can feel relieved and insulted at the same time?!'"

WINNING MOVES:
> I think the last line of the story says it all –we can feel relieved and insulted at the same time when we do not get offered a position. It's like not being invited to a party that you didn't want to go to in the first place.

Cosmic cognitive dissonance

"When thinking about job interviews, two from my past immediately came to mind. In one I was interviewing under buzzing florescent lights that caused my brain to go marginally epileptic, thereby triggering a number of incoherent answers. (Didn't get that job.) The other involved a dining hall manager who screened female job applicants for their willingness to spend quality time with him personally. (I got the job but didn't actually have to put out.) Those are from my youth. The following is more recent.

Several years ago I went to an interview for which I had high hopes. The job paid well, I believed in the work, and I was a friend of the interviewer/

hirer. In addition, I thought I was well prepared for the job by my 30 year work history.

The position I was applying for was a coordinator/program manager. The role involved pulling a community together, networking, and establishing collaboration that created a strong, well-defined entity that could advocate its needs and be coherent to funders and government entities. I was looking forward to my people skills carrying the day. However, when I arrived for the interview there was no effort made to talk with me. Instead, they immediately gave me the choice to tackle one of two computer-based tasks to be completed in isolation.

One task was to create an Excel spreadsheet from a mound of non-contextualized data. The other was to create a Word document clustering an extensive list of items by category and importance. The assignments completely threw me off my stride. This was not supposed to be an admin nor an IT position. The skill set I imagined to be vital to this job had no relationship with the tasks before me. However, I was too afraid to ask why they wanted me to do this. I assumed that asking 'why' would betray a foundational ignorance that would jeopardize my chance at landing the position. So I accepted the idea that to get to the actual interview, I had to first run this gauntlet of computer-based tasks.

I chose the Word based activity because of my greater familiarity with the software. I sweated it out for a half hour and produced a document. When I was done, they finally interviewed me, thanked me, and said goodbye. Later I was offered the position.

I should have seen the signals! On my first day, my boss insisted the whole office watch her fret and rant over an unmet deadline based on a mystery task for nigh on to an hour after closing time. Thinking this was not within my portfolio, I slipped out after 45 minutes. The next day she furiously chewed me out. Things went downhill from there. I was half fired/half quit eleven months later. My entire tenure there – from the interview through the last day on the job – was one cosmic cognitive dissonance! *Lesson learned*: if it walks like a duck…"

> **WINNING MOVES:**
> Experiencing cognitive dissonance, tension caused by holding two opposing beliefs at the same time, can be a red flag during an interview. And when our interview cosmos has strange vibes, it's possible the workplace galaxy will hold the same strange vibes. Interviewee beware...there may indeed be little green men out there.

How'd mom do?

"We were interviewing for a teller position and made a decision to make an offer to a young woman. When I called her home, a child answered. I asked to speak to his mother and he surprised me by saying, 'Did my mom get the job? Did my mom get the job?' He sounded so eager that I wanted to tell him 'yes,' but I could hardly let him relate the message to his mother. Instead I had to say, 'Well, I think I need to talk to your mom.'

Since she became a long-time employee, I had the pleasure of seeing her son from time to time as he grew up. But my fondest memory remains of him as a small child answering the phone, all excited about the prospect of his mother getting the job."

> **WINNING MOVES:**
> Although this story occurred *after* the interview, it's one of the pieces that completed the hiring loop. We sometimes forget that the way the decision is presented can be important. I've had people tell me that the offer was a let-down because there was no *congratulations*; rather the conversation became the beginning of negotiations. How people are brought on board and brought up-to-speed for the position is a part of the recruiting and hiring process and can greatly influence a new employee's attitude toward their job.

Water Bottle Abacus

"We conduct very informal interviews when we hire adjunct faculty at our college. Since there are four of us in our department, we all attend each interview, which is actually done in two sessions. The first is a get-to-know the applicant session, and the second is reserved for those who we decide to move forward. The problem is that, since we have to all agree on who to move forward to the second phase, we must ask the successful applicants to come back a second time, and this is usually seen as an inconvenience to the applicants.

One day the four of us had a bright idea. We conduct our interviews in a room that has a table with water bottles in the center. To speed up the decision-making process, we agreed that, if we really liked the applicant, then, as soon as each of the four of us made the decision that we'd invite the person to the second phase, we would take a bottle of water from the center of the table and put it in front of us. If at some point in the interview, all four had taken a bottle, that meant that we all wanted to move to the second phase and we would immediately tell the applicant that we were interested and ask the applicant if they'd like to move forward. But if even one of the four of us had not taken a bottle, we'd just end the interview and thank the applicant for interviewing with us.

During the next interview, one by one, each of us being so impressed with the interviewee, we each took a bottle of water until all four of us had one in front of us. Aha! It worked perfectly!

When we immediately told the interviewee that we were interested in moving forward and asked him if he was interested in discussing the position in more detail, he said *'Are you sure you don't want to talk with each other with me out of the room first?'* Then he reached for a bottle of water, and we broke into laughter. He didn't know it, but he was voting for himself!"

WINNING MOVES:

I gave this story the title "water bottle abacus" because the interviewers identified a numeric tool to calculate responses quickly and without using words or modern technology. An unusual yet simple way of communicating a complex thought. It's no wonder the interviewee was surprised by the speed of their decision making.

The Polygraph

"It takes a couple of weeks to get through the first part of the process when applying to be a fire fighter in my state. There is a written test that asks general aptitude questions, and you have to score close to 100 percent. You also have to meet the physical fitness requirements and pass the background check. Then you get to the polygraph. Sometimes there is also an interview, but I went straight to the polygraph.

I knew people who had taken the polygraph, told the truth but didn't get the job as well as people who told the truth and did get the job. I also knew of people who had lied and failed and lied and passed. I heard from different people about how to take it and pass. They said the tool tests the fear factor and that what they try to do is to get you to change your answers. I was also told that one technique is to put a tack in your shoe so that your pain registers the same on the screen for all of the questions. But if they catch you with a tack in your shoe, you fail.

They ask three kinds of questions. Neutral questions such as your name or the number of lights in the room, background questions – mostly about drug use and drinking. They get very specific about this. Like if you've ever smoked pot, then how many times. Or, if you've ever drank and drove. If you say 'yes' then they want details. And then there are character questions, like if you have ever lied to your boss or wife. Although I knew I didn't have anything to hide, I decided ahead of time that whatever I said I was going to give the same answer every time they asked.

The set-up was a small, white room with me looking straight ahead, staring at the wall. The woman administering the test was at a desk off to one side. Since I couldn't move, she was staring at the side of my face for the entire test. The first thing they do is tell you what questions they are going to ask to calm your nerves. Then they hook you up. There's the pad you sit on. If you bunch up your butt cheeks or move your feet, that's a sign that you might be lying. Then they put a band around your chest to monitor your breathing. Then there's a finger monitor to check your heart rate.

Just getting hooked up was pretty intense. And since before we got started I'd been told that I nodded my head a lot and shouldn't do that during the test, all I could think about was not to nod my head.

The woman then asked the same questions she'd told me she would, but in a different order. She would ask a question, pause, have me respond, then wait a minute to let the baseline come back. This went on for 10-15 minutes. Then we went through the questions two more times.

I didn't actually lie, but I focused on being consistent rather than thinking about the specific details. I mean, I'm human, so I probably lied to my boss at some point, but I couldn't remember a time, so I said 'no.' Every time they asked the question, I said 'no.' It was easier than trying to explain what *might* have happened and then say the same thing over and over.

Taking the polygraph was quite an experience, and not very many made it through, but I'm glad I did. I like my job."

WINNING MOVES:

The above story came from a former Marine. Like many vets he was facing the issue of how to make the transition to a job market that wasn't necessarily receptive to the argument about "transferable skills." So when he decided to apply to become a fire fighter, he carefully and successfully researched the hiring process and overcame a hurdle that many have not managed to overcome.

Conclusion:

"Accidents" occur because you don't anticipate that something is about to happen. Although you can do a lot to prevent accidents, you can never avoid them completely. The same is true of surprises or unexpected twists during an interview. No matter how much you try to anticipate what might come up, there is no way you can anticipate every possibility. The options are as varied as the people involved. The key is to try to stay calm in the moment, and afterwards, if the worst happens, try not to beat yourself up too much. Playing *woulda, coulda, shoulda* doesn't make it go away and can have a negative impact on your self-confidence at a time when you need to be at your best.

LESSONS LEARNED THE EASY WAY
(Through Someone Else's Experience)

The Unexpected: You can and should plan carefully for an interview, but there is no way you can anticipate everything that could possibly happen. Accept that fact and don't second-guess yourself after the fact.

- *Know thyself…as much as possible.*
  We all have blind spots, things others may know about us that we don't know about ourselves. And learning about a blind spot during an interview can be painful. But life is a journey of learning. Ask for feedback, integrate the self-knowledge into your consciousness, and move on.

- *When in doubt about the direction of the conversation, ask a question.*
  "Would you please repeat the question?" "Would you like me to discuss…?" "Would you like me to tell you about a time when…?" Asking questions keeps you from making statements you will regret. They may also help you redirect the conversation to something you feel more comfortable with. And, finally, questions give you time to think and re-group. Never underestimate the power of the question.

- *Don't personalize rejection.*
  As I've said before, it's easy to get hung up on being the perfect fit for the job description. But the job description is only a small part of the whole. There may be unstated expectations. Or you may look or sound like someone the hiring manager dislikes. Interviews can be fluky; people aren't always consistent or predictable. That's life.

- *Trust your instincts. Or at least ask questions to verify or disprove them.*
  When we want a job, the tendency is to ignore red flags during the interview. We can rationalize, ignore, and deny. Then, later on, we

say: "I should have known..." One way to explore your concerns is to share them with someone who will give you honest feedback. If you decide to proceed in spite of the warnings, you will at least go into the new position prepared for some challenges.

8
Mirth and Missteps

Tilt-shift photography refers to using a type of lens to experiment with perspective and simulate miniature scenes, usually from above. I've often thought that the ability to view interviews through a tilt-shift lens would be very helpful. You could rise above the narrow focus of participant and capture a wide angle view of the event, experiencing what both interviewers and interviewees are seeing at a particular moment in time.

In the following stories you can use your internal tilt-shift lens to envision the miniature scenes that tell stories of mirth and missteps. Mirth because they are amusing, and missteps that sometimes turn out to be the right step after all. But not always–.

You can't necessarily tell from reading the following stories, but they represent a broad spectrum of industries, including an international gaming company, an environmental engineering firm, a nonprofit, a small start-up, a bank, a national retail store, and a city agency. Although the companies are distinct from one another, the experiences of the people involved could have happened in any organization, large or small, public or private, for-profit or nonprofit. Interviews are about the people in the organizations, and people share both common values and foibles.

Read the large print

"As a hiring manager, you want candidates to do well. But sometimes that just isn't meant to be. I was interviewing a candidate whose only experience was that of an elementary school teacher. She wanted to move from the public schools to corporate America, but she struggled to translate her teaching experience into the requirements of the corporate position. I tried to encourage her to do just that, to explain how her current skill set would make her a qualified candidate for the training position I had described. She tried and got a little closer, so I decided to help her along by giving her a specific example to address.

'*What steps would you take to make participants in a workshop feel at ease?*' I asked.

'*I would write my name in big, clear letters on the chalkboard so that everyone would know that my name is Mrs._____.*'

She did not get the job."

> **WINNING MOVES:**
> If you've ever made a career change, you can probably empathize with the woman in this story at the same time that you are shaking your head at the Pavlovian nature of her response. Kudos to the interviewer for trying to help her out.

Impressing the right person

"I was the HR manager for an environmental engineering firm, and we were hiring for a field tech, entry level position. A guy in his 40s applied. He was trying to make a transition from another line of work. He made the case that he had been in charge in his last position and knew how to handle responsibility under challenging circumstances. On the one hand I believed him, but he wasn't exactly the person I'd been looking for. Fortunately, he was persistent, but not in an obnoxious way.

You'd think that skill sets and proven experience would be enough. But it all boiled down to the candidate impressing the right person to prove that he deserved a chance. In this instance, I was the person he needed to impress, and he did so by not giving up when he saw I was hesitant about his experience. So, he got his chance. I passed his name along to the hiring manager, and he got the job."

WINNING MOVES:
This is the kind of interviewer we all want to find across from us at the table, someone willing to see potential rather than holding fast to a bullet point on a job description. On the other hand, as a hiring manager expected to find someone who can get up to speed immediately, you may not feel you have the luxury of taking a chance on someone who doesn't meet all of the experience requirements set forth in the job description. Spending some time and effort learning how to assess and/or describe comparable skill sets can be beneficial to those on both sides of the interview table.

The long wait

"We had a candidate come for an interview a few minutes early, and the recruiter left him in a chair outside of the interview room. I saw him waiting there and went over to reassure him that we knew he was there. He stood up and introduced himself: '*Hi, I'm Michael...*'

When I finally got all of the interviewers rounded up, I returned to get him. He stood up and with an absolutely straight face said, '*Hi, I'm still Michael...*' That little bit of dry humor was enough to make me take notice and appreciate him."

WINNING MOVES:

There are some experts on the interview process who advise against use of humor. Granted we don't all laugh at the same things, but if a sense of humor is one of your strengths or something you value in the workplace, then I say "go for it." Within limits. And with your antennae out to make sure your humor isn't off-putting. It's also important to remember that interviewers may assume the mantle of seriousness to ensure fairness and consistency of process. That may or may not be indicative of what the organization's culture is like. Of course, it's also possible that they may seem receptive and laugh at your jokes and still not hire you.

Son!

"I once landed a job in a fifteen minute interview. It wasn't that I was the best qualified or the best fit, but the interviewer liked me. She told me that she wanted her son to be more like me. Then she offered me the job. Unfortunately, it only lasted two weeks. At that time, I got a better offer where I was appreciated for my skill set and not for my 'son' appeal. I bet she no longer wants her son to be more like me!"

WINNING MOVES:

What can I say – kids can sometimes be a disappointment.

You gotta be kidding me

"We were slowly working our way through the list of candidates whose resumes had made it to the interview pool for a corporate communications position. We had a lot to choose from, and they all looked good on paper.

When the first person came into the room my thought was 'right on.' Let's call her Betty. Betty looked professional and made a great first impression. Everyone seemed comfortable, including Betty, and the interview got off to a good start. She had reasonable answers for the first couple of questions, and then I asked a more in-depth question regarding past experiences and she said, '*Now what position is this interview for?*' Betty went on to say that she had applied for so many jobs that she was getting them mixed up.

NEXT...

Then my VP and I interviewed another professional appearing woman named Gretchen for the same position. Gretchen immediately took over the conversation, began asking *us* questions, and starting telling us how she was going to run the department. My boss kicked me under the table while looking out the window. It was time to thank Gretchen and tell her good luck!

I walked away from both interviews thinking, 'you gotta be kidding me.' They had both flunked interview 101, and I had learned more than I wanted to know about the sometimes startling disconnect between a resume and its writer."

WINNING MOVES:

Resumes have gone from a chronicle of past job experiences to an art form, a science, and a profession. I saw an ad recently for services that can give you a list of the top ten words to use for online resumes in different professions. The thought that getting your resume reviewed is dependent on knowing the right buzz words may be a bit depressing, but then landing a job has always been a competitive endeavor. It's just that the rules of the game have changed and in the current economy the stakes are higher. So, dust off your resume writing skills, take a deep breath, and keep sending them out. Just try to remember who you're talking to when you get that interview!

YOUR job

"Some time ago I interviewed someone and at one point asked what I assumed to be a pretty fair question under the circumstances: '*Where do you see yourself in five years?*' The candidate responded: '*With your job.*'

When I informed her that I wasn't planning on leaving and asked if she had any other hopes and dreams for five years down the road, she repeated: '*I want your job within five years.*'

Needless to say I didn't hire her."

> **WINNING MOVES:**
> Writing in his career center blog, Matt Youngquist offered the following question as his way of diagnosing how somebody did in a job interview: "*What did you learn about the needs, challenges and expectations of the hiring manager that you didn't know before you walked into the interview?*" How do you think the above interviewee would have (or could have) responded? Maybe she ought to check out Matt's blog.

How old are you?

"The president of the board called to set up an interview with me. My child answered the telephone, and when I got on the line, the first question he asked was, '*Was that your child who answered?*' I told him it was. Then he asked, '*So, how old are you?*'

I politely but firmly informed the president of the board that there were certain kinds of questions that were illegal to ask. In response, he said: '*Well, I guess I'll see how old you are when we meet.*'

That should have been a clue as to what I was getting into, but I really wanted a job, and that job in particular. I lasted a little over a year–."

> **WINNING MOVES:**
> Since her age was probably not an issue for the position, this board member was using his authority to let her know that not only did he expect his questions to be answered, but he had to have the last word. One thing for sure, she was a year older when she left that position for another job.

Brownies anyone?

"I heard a story about someone who applied for an HR job and baked brownies for the team interviewing her. They had a good laugh at her expense, scoffing that she must have confused an interview with a potluck. She didn't get the job; but not because of the brownies. They were apparently quite tasty."

> **WINNING MOVES:**
> I'm reminded of something an executive recruiter once said: "Apparently some human resource managers don't appreciate having interview questions answered through interpretive dance." Or, in this instance, through a mistaken belief that everyone can be enticed by chocolate.

Conclusion:

In each of the above stories, one can imagine a Norman Rockwell depiction of the interview frozen in time, a miniature scene representing a slice of American business life. Each a perfect cover for the *Saturday Evening Post* of yesteryear.

Unfortunately, you don't always know when you've made a misstep during an interview. As the interviewee, all you know for sure is whether you get the job or not. And as the interviewer, if no one makes a formal complaint, you may not realize or care that you stepped over a line. But if you could rise above the interview with your wide angle lens, you might be able to see and understand everything.

LESSONS LEARNED THE EASY WAY
(Through Someone Else's Experience)

Missteps: Mistakes are in the eye of the beholder. Sometimes you don't know that you've made one until after the fact. Other times you may never know. But someone does–.

- *Make sure you understand the question or request before responding.*
  Of course the misstep occurs when you don't realize that you misunderstood the question or request before responding. So if you are at all uncertain, ask for clarification.

- *If you are the interviewer, give comparable experience a chance.*
  Some people believe that you should hire for attitude and train for skills, whereas others are convinced that you need to hire someone who has already done the job so they can hit the ground running. Job titles don't always tell the full story. By giving "comparable experience a chance" I simply mean allowing the person to explain the kinds of competencies and skills they have that caused them to apply for the job in the first place.

- *If you are the interviewee, be prepared to explain why your skills are a good match for the position.*
  Don't begin by saying, "I've never actually been in this kind of a position before, but…" Rather, make a list of the kinds of tasks you've done and skills you have and be prepared to talk about them at the appropriate time.

- *Use humor sparingly.*
  Too much joking around can be seen as nervousness or lack of professionalism. Some interview experts caution against *any* use of

humor, but use of humor can lighten the mood and make people feel more at ease. Just don't overdo it.

- *Don't try to impress hiring managers by telling them what you would do when you get the job.*
  It's tempting to use your past experience to talk about what you could do for a new employer. And sometimes interviewees are asked what they would do "if"–. But even when asked, it's best to temper your response with an acknowledgment that there's a lot of background needed before making final recommendations. The rule of thumb is that it takes about three months to really understand a new organization and its culture. Be prepared to state up front what you would expect to do during that time to become an effective change agent.

9

No Dead Air in This Interview!

"Dead air" is an unintended interruption in a radio broadcast during which no sound is transmitted, or, in the case of television, a blank screen appears. It isn't just the professional broadcaster who considers dead air as one of the worst things that can occur. Somewhere buried deep in the psyche of most of us is the fear of dead air space at a time when we feel we ought to be saying something wise or clever or perceptive. Like during an interview. Ironically, this fear often results in the opposite thing happening – too much talk.

People talk too much for all sorts of reasons - nervousness, the thrill of having a captive audience, being unaware of nonverbal cues to get them to shut up, and even as a power play. All of these possibilities are reflected in the following stories. Someone is talking too much, and it isn't always the interviewee.

I know stuff—

"It was a telephone screening interview: my first. Although I didn't realize exactly what it was at the time. For more than 20 years I had been the interviewer of people who had been prescreened for me, but I didn't know enough about prescreening to recognize that when I applied for a particular job, I was going to be prescreened!

Since I assumed the telephone interview was going to be with a knowledgeable staff person, I prepared thoroughly for what I was told via email would be a 45-60 minute interview. When the person called at the appointed time, she immediately said the interview would be only 20 minutes. So to cover all of the information I had prepared for a longer interview, I spoke quickly and dominated the conversation, almost without interruption. I also asked nuanced, detailed questions to show off my knowledge to someone I assumed to be a peer.

At the 20 minute mark she interrupted to thank me. In response, I thanked her and said that I had so much more to discuss.

Needless to say, I never got an opportunity for more discussion. I didn't get a call-back."

> **WINNING MOVES:**
> Focusing on what you want to get across rather than paying attention to the person asking the questions is never a good idea. That's the downside of over-preparation – we get the feeling that everything we have to tell the interviewer is important. Letting go of your own agenda but still getting in enough detail to demonstrate your experience and enthusiasm is a delicate balancing act that requires both preparation and awareness of the impact you are having in the moment.

Speak up!

"Early in my career as a newly minted environmental scientist, I tagged along on a client interview. It was my opportunity to learn from the master, a senior consultant who supposedly knew how to get results. However, early in the conversation I could tell that the senior consultant wasn't listening to the client, or else he didn't understand the client's perspective. In either case, the senior consultant kept selling while the client kept asking questions that weren't being answered to his satisfaction, and I just kept my mouth shut.

Needless to say, we didn't get the project. But that is how I learned a very important lesson. Sometimes keeping your mouth shut is not the best option. The ability to speak up and re-direct a conversation with questions can be a valuable asset. And it's one I'm still learning..."

WINNING MOVES:

If you are doing too much talking, you aren't listening. And if you are present when someone else is on this path to self-destruction, you can help them out, as suggested by the author of the above story, by interrupting with a question that moves the conversation in a new direction. But there is a danger in that approach, too. Often times the person doing all of the talking will not take the hint and may simply see you as being rude for interrupting. You need to carefully weigh the options and consequences before jumping in to save someone. Learning from the mistakes of others is painful to watch, but it may be the best alternative.

Big cats

"I was interviewing for a senior level leadership development role at a local office of an international telecomm-wireless firm. The hiring manager/interviewer had just been hired and hadn't yet relocated from the Midwest. Unfortunately, he was more interested in talking about himself and his new role than in learning about me. He told me about his background, his family, his values, and about being really into 'big cats'– tigers, leopards, jaguars, and the like. In addition, he kept fiddling with his new Blackberry and actually began loading it during the interview because he was so excited to start using it.

At the time I thought that he might not have been interested in me as a serious candidate, but he called me back for a 2nd interview. This time it included his department members. Although I was pretty sure I did not want to work for him, I went to the 2nd interview partly as a networking opportunity. Leadership and Organizational Development are small professional fields and it's good to increase your circle of contacts. Besides, I was curious to meet the people who had hired him to be over leadership development when he didn't even know how to conduct an employment interview.

I wasn't too surprised on the day of my 2nd interview to find that he hadn't made his flight back to the main office after visiting family over the weekend. His coworkers were stressed because he was supposed to lead an important presentation that afternoon for his new organization, a presentation that was to introduce him as the new senior leader. And his team didn't know what he had planned to present, so they didn't feel like they could step in and cover for him.

Clearly it was difficult for everyone to focus on my 2nd interview. But we got through it. And I was neither surprised nor disappointed to receive word that the position I'd interviewed for had been cut from the budget before it was filled."

WINNING MOVES:

The interviewer who talks too much obviously does not get a sense of what the interviewee has to offer. Unfortunately, most interviewers who talk too much are unaware of the problem because they are enjoying themselves. Although the interviewee can jump in and offer information they feel is critical to getting hired, they may be better off pumping the ego of the interviewer by being the world's best listener. It's a judgment call that can only be made in the moment.

Look at what WE do

"When I go to an interview I always want to be prepared. But for one interview I should have slept another hour instead. The interviewer spent our time by leafing through the company's organization chart and strategic plan...a HUGE binder full of information and details. All I had to do was appear interested and ask an occasional question. The interviewer got a chance to talk and be listened to, but learned nothing about me."

WINNING MOVES:

> Again, it's a matter of whether you try to change the flow of the interview or simply "appear interested." If you accept the situation for what it is, at least you will score high on listening skills! And the speaker won't hear anything that he or she doesn't like–.

Clueless

"We conducted two different interviews where the reaction to the candidates was very negative.

In the first, the candidate talked and talked and talked. She seemed completely unaware that the interviewers – all but one – were feeling frustrated by the fact that not only was she talking too much, but she wasn't answering the questions appropriately. But, it only took one person, the individual to whom the woman would report, to respond positively. So in this instance, being clueless wasn't a problem. She got the job.

In the second situation, the interviewers were so turned off by the candidate that they literally turned away from the person being interviewed. They actually shifted their chairs, whether consciously or unconsciously I'm not sure. From time to time they would glance back at the candidate as though trying to be polite by feigning engagement. The candidate didn't appear to notice. And in this case, the candidate was not offered the job."

WINNING MOVES:

Wouldn't you like to be at the back of the room and hold up cue cards that say things like, "It's your turn to listen" or "Hello – check out the body language of the other people in the room." Of course, it's always possible that you are seeing some unusual behavior in the interviewee brought about by fear and discomfort. And if you told the story from the interviewee's point of view, you might feel sympathy for their situation.

You're hired – whether you want to be or not

"It was a pretty big job – managing fifteen people as the operations manager over the call center, tax reporting and client support for three separate Mutual Fund/Hedge Fund companies. I was young. I was flattered. And I was hired before I had a chance to think whether this was a good move or not.

The hiring manager called me in, asked a couple of basic questions, and then started talking. And talking. And talking. Telling me what a good opportunity this was. What a great job it was. Sell, sell, sell. Then she left the room and I overheard her on the telephone: '*I found our guy...can you come down and meet him?*' That was how quickly it happened. I never even had a chance to say if I was interested in the position.

I accepted the offer, but I learned an important lesson: never accept a job from a hiring manager that doesn't earn your respect up front, because that's not likely to change when they become your boss. Was it the great job that I'd been promised? In some ways. But the interview set the tone for the position and for the relationship. That didn't change.

Another lesson I learned over the years is that getting a job isn't always as easy as that!"

WINNING MOVES:

Determining when an interview is indicative of what working at the company would be like is difficult. In large companies, recruiters have an image they want to project. Even in small companies everyone can be on their very best behavior. But if the person doing the interview is the one you will be working for, then you need to trust your instincts. Or you may end up in a situation like the interviewee of this story.

Flying at 500 feet

"One time I was sitting on an interview panel for a VP of Lending position. The interview dragged out for two and a half hours because the candidate wouldn't stop talking! It was absolutely ridiculous. The candidate kept asking questions that were way too detailed about the most minute aspects of the job. And every time they were asked about how they would handle a particular system or process, they would go into great detail about their background with the program or process. They were absolutely incapable of staying at the 30,000 foot level."

WINNING MOVES:

And so they talked themselves out of the position–. NOT a winning move.

Yakety yak

"When you are looking for someone to interact with the public, you can be misled by the fact that the person you are interviewing is chatty and friendly. It is easy to assume that being outgoing equates with good customer service. On the other hand, if someone talks and talks and talks during an interview, that should be a red flag. It just may mean that they never listen. We interviewed a presentable young woman who talked too much, but she was experienced and seemed to have a pleasant personality. So we hired her. It's amazing that she listened long enough to get the message when we finally decided to let her go."

> **WINNING MOVES:**
> In the song by The Coasters from the late 50's, the theme is "Yakety yak; don't talk back." In this instance, no one was getting orders – they didn't stop talking long enough to hear any!

Silence is golden; duct tape is silver

"You know how sometimes you meet someone and right away feel put off? Well, that's how I felt when I met the hiring manager for a position I had been recommended for by a friend and colleague. I didn't want to make a bad impression and embarrass my friend, but I was uncomfortable from the get-go. And it got immediately worse when she informed me that we didn't have a room reserved for the interview, so we would have to find one.

The company was a large one, and the building was a maze of hallways and work areas. We started wandering down hallway after hallway peering in through tiny windows to see whether the room was vacant. This went on and on and on.

When I get uncomfortable or nervous I have a tendency to babble. And I was both uncomfortable and nervous, so I started trying to make small talk. I asked about the building, how long the company had been at the headquarters, how many people were housed there, etcetera. She gave me brief, unenthusiastic answers. Then suddenly she stopped in the middle of the hallway, turned to me and asked, *'What's with this fascination about the building?'*

I can't tell you exactly what I said, but it didn't make things better. And even today I'm not sure there was a 'right' answer to that question. Maybe she was overreacting because she had failed to reserve a room and we were spending far too much time searching for one. I'll never know. We did finally find a space to talk, but we ended our interview at the allotted time even though we started over 20 minutes late! The only thing I did right was to keep my mouth shut as we made our way back to the building's entrance.

All she told my friend was that I wasn't the right person for the job. End of story."

WINNING MOVES:

There is a popular picture that depicts a happy face with duct tape across the mouth and the saying: *"Silence is golden. Duct tape is silver."* Silence may be golden, but it can also be interpreted as lack of engagement. In situations like the above, it's hard to know whether it would have been better to do the room search in silence. Maybe the small talk topic was the problem. Although perhaps it's a moot question because it doesn't seem like it would have been a good boss-employee fit in any case.

Conclusion:

How much information should you provide during an interview? How much should you say about a particular project or example? How many questions should you ask? These are all decisions that are situation specific. You can give exactly the same response in two different interviews and impress one set of interviewers and turn off the other. Listening carefully to what is being asked of you and paying careful attention to nonverbal cues can go a long way toward finding that balance between too much and too little talk. You don't want dead air, but you also don't want to overwhelm the airwaves.

LESSONS LEARNED THE EASY WAY
(Through Someone Else's Experience)

Talking too much: Knowing when to listen and when to talk is a valuable skill. Especially in an interview.

- *No one knows what you planned to say except you.*
  Your planning for an interview should include practice in answering questions you anticipate you will be asked. But you can't count on having things turn out exactly as planned. Be prepared to make succinct answers or to lengthen answers by using examples. And remember – you can't get it wrong; no one heard your practice sessions but you.

- *Augment listening with questions.*
  If you find yourself in a situation where the interviewer seems to want to do most of the talking, occasionally ask a question to indicate that you are an active listener. And be prepared to jump in when given the opportunity.

  Also, if the person doing all of the talking is the individual you would report to, you might want to think twice about the position. Or, if you get the opportunity to talk to other direct reports, ask questions to find out more about their management style. Sometimes managers are different in interviews than in day-to-day operations.

- *Avoid talking too much.*
  That sounds like simple advice, but it can be difficult to gauge how much is too much. Usually listeners will give nonverbal clues, but some people are very good at hiding their displeasure. If in doubt, pause and ask, "Would you like me to elaborate?" If they say "no," that's a clue.

- *Ask interviewers about the level of detail they want when asked a question.* If you aren't sure whether the question requires a strategic or tactical response, ask. They might not be sure themselves. A safe approach if they remain unclear is to describe your strategy or process and ask if they would like examples.

10
Semper Gumby

Marine Corps Captain Jay Farmer is credited with the first use of the phrase Semper Gumby, "always flexible." He had a Gumby toy mounted on a compass in the helicopter he flew. Remember Gumby? A green plastic, flexible, smiling humanoid figure that you could bend into almost any shape, over and over. Although even Gumby had its limits. If you bent one back and forth enough times, the wire inside could break through the plastic. But the smile never went away.

Flexibility is usually a good quality for an interviewee to have. It's a mental attitude that enables you to adapt to whatever is thrown your way during the interview. But sometimes the wire pokes through no matter how hard you try.

The twelve stories in this chapter look at the issue of flexibility from different angles. In one instance, someone totally changes his approach to an interview based on an encounter in the parking lot. Another reacts immediately to feedback and sets themselves up for success. In several other stories, interviewees cope with the lack of flexibility on the part of the person in control of the conversation. One person even pushes back on an inflexible attitude. Finally, a number of candidates learn the hard way that flexibility may be a positive trait, but it doesn't always pay off.

You have one minute

"Just before I graduated from college I got an interview with one of the big consulting firms. The recruiter had scheduled round one interviews at fifteen minute intervals. My interview was the first one after lunch.

The recruiter was *ten minutes* late. That meant there were *five minutes* remaining for my interview if he was going to stay on schedule. Then he informed me that he had not received my resume, so I gave him the extra copy I had brought with me. He read it for *four minutes*. That left *one minute* for a single question and short response, while he kept checking his watch. Then the interview was over. He thanked me and efficiently moved on to his next candidate. On time.

I did not get invited to round two."

> **WINNING MOVES:**
> I think Gumby needed to flex a little more.

Damn good

"I already was in an HR director position but was applying for another director position. I was only 30 at the time, and the interviewer was much older. Apparently he felt like I shouldn't already be a director at my age and was trying to figure out how I had managed it. In a totally HR inappropriate way he asked: '*How did you get ahead so fast? Who'd you sleep with?*'

For once in my life I had a quick answer: '*I didn't sleep with anyone; I'm just damn good!*'

And I got the job."

> **WINNING MOVES:**
> Gumby rocks!

Times a-changin'

"It was 1992. I was in graduate school, had two kids, and needed to bring in some more money. So when I heard that a computer retailer was looking for part-time sales help, I decided to apply. I didn't have any certifications, but I felt like I was ahead of the curve on computers and computer networking, so it seemed worth a shot.

I arrived early. While I was waiting to pull into a parking spot, I saw a guy run out to a car, get in, and immediately back out of the spot. He was heading straight for me. I honked and we both swerved. When we got out to see whether we'd actually scraped each other, there didn't seem to be any damage. The guy explained that he was upset because he'd just been fired – from the same company I was there to apply with. We talked for about half an hour. He'd been the director of their PC network sales. He was Microsoft network certified and had several other certifications as well. He told me that their complaint was that he wasn't nice to people. He had the technical knowledge but had poor customer service skills.

If you remember what it was like then, there weren't computers on every desk; the day of key boards and green screens connected to big computers was just coming to an end. Computers and computer networking was on the brink of becoming big business.

When the interviewer came out to greet me, he asked if I was there about the part-time sales position. I said that what I was really interested in was networks. I added that I felt it was important to tell the story of networks better. That you have to sell computer based PC networks different from mainframes. That people currently in charge of information technology didn't know or want to know about the technical side of things; they just wanted to know how to connect their work needs with technical solutions and do things that made sense. When he asked if I had any certifications, I said that you could always hire technical people to take care of the technical side of things.

When I left the interview I was their new director of PC network sales.

Later I found out that the guy they fired had ticked off the Sr. VP of one of their long-time, important clients. I also discovered that I was right about what clients wanted. I became the front guy, visiting clients and doing needs assessments. The clients were pleased not to have to talk with techies, and I had two techies back at the office who were more than happy to contribute their expertise as needed. On a commission basis, with four or five clients a month, it turned out to be a great job for a student."

WINNING MOVES:
> This story illustrates the ultimate in flexibility. And it reminds me of something Yogi Berra said: *"If you come to a fork in the road, take it."*

I Volunteer

"We were hiring for a youth employment program leader and had a lot of outstanding applicants with considerable experience in the field. This is what I explained to a very personable, energetic young woman who was very interested in the job but just didn't have the right credentials. Yes, she was a highly qualified professional with a varied background and lots of potential. But when you are weighing potential against tried and true, it makes sense to go with the latter.

Since she was an impressive person who seemed genuinely interested in the position, I decided to give her some advice. I told her that one way to get into the area was to volunteer to do the type of work she was interested in eventually doing for pay. She thanked me and left my office.

Moments later there was a knock on my door. She came back in and offered her services as a volunteer!

Within a couple of weeks we had a part-time position become available. She applied for and got that. And it wasn't all that long until I got a promotion and she landed my job. I had obviously given her very good advice."

WINNING MOVES:
It's nice to read a success story about someone who manages to use flexibility and persistence to their advantage and break into a new field. Kudos to both the advice giver and to the woman who was smart enough to listen to the advice.

Resume critique

"My interview with the hiring manager for an OD (organization development) manager level position went well. Then I was asked back to talk to the VP of Operations, a potential internal client. He had my resume on the table in front of him. Instead of a conversation or questions I got a critique of my resume.

He told me he was looking for numbers, dollars, and metrics, like he would expect to see in an operational resume. He lectured me about how I should know better. I met his challenges by explaining how I work and the qualitative/behavioral results I achieve. When I left, I was feeling fairly horrible.

I always wondered who they offered the job to before they had to fall back and take me!"

WINNING MOVES:
A bad interview experience can linger, even if you are offered the position. In their book *Life 101*, John-Roger and Peter McWilliams offer good advice for a situation like this: *"Whenever he thought about it he felt terrible. And so, at last, he came to a fateful decision. He decided not to think about it."*

Bullets?!

"It wasn't actually a job interview, but it was a type of interview. I had submitted a proposal based on guidelines provided by the 'interviewer' and was hoping to get the individual (let's call him 'Uptight Ted') to represent me. Even though Uptight Ted had asked me to call, he couldn't at first remember who I was. When he finally put it together, the real reason for granting the interview came to the surface.

'Instead of a bulleted list, you used numbers,' he complained. *'Obviously you don't know how to follow directions.'*

- He then launched off on all of the non-substantive flaws in my proposal.
- His goal seemed to be to chastise me for not specifically following his directions in putting the proposal together.
- He had no intention of talking about anything else.
- I got off of the telephone as quickly as I could.

The above bulleted list is dedicated to Uptight Ted."

> **WINNING MOVES:**
> I think Uptight Ted needs a little love from Gumby.

What are you doing here?

"When you are looking for a job you are usually very good about remembering the date and time of an interview that you are hoping results in employment. So when I showed up for a scheduled interview, I was surprised when the assistant and the person who had originally called me to schedule the interview both asked: *'What are you doing here?'*

They said that the interview had been rescheduled; in fact, she claimed that we had talked about the rescheduling. (I *think* I would have remembered a little detail like that.) She then rescheduled me to a different day that could accommodate me and the hiring manager. I should have walked away at that point because I was certain that she would not tell the hiring manager that it was not ME who got the date wrong. In retrospect, that was probably a huge red flag.

Fast forward to interview day... During my interview with the hiring manager, she took two calls from her cell phone and didn't write down a thing while I was answering her questions. She became so rude that I was convinced she just wanted me to leave. Instead I took every minute of the time allotted (and a little more) to ask insane questions about super specific things just to annoy. It seemed the least I could do under the circumstances."

WINNING MOVES:
Flexibility and rolling over are two different things. Sometimes you need to let the wires poke through. Just a little. For your own sense of satisfaction and closure. And for the story, of course.

Not a good fit

"Sometimes the phrase 'not a good fit' is simply a way of saying that the reasons for you not getting the job are either complicated or uncomfortable to talk about. But in this case, it was completely accurate.

When the recruiter contacted me about the position I explained that I was surprised because the job was not like anything I had ever done before. She told me that it didn't matter because I had comparable skills and would be able to get up to speed quickly. I had my doubts, but I was looking for a change, so I went to the interview.

It was clear very early in the interview that I didn't have the experience they were looking for. One look at my resume should have told them that, but they continued to drive home the point that I wasn't a good fit. I tried to tell them what the recruiter had told me, but they weren't interested.

I left feeling as though I had been unfairly treated. In retrospect, I can see both sides. Clearly there are transferable skills, especially when you are at the management level. But in today's fast-paced business environment, who has the luxury of hiring someone who will take time to come up to speed? I just wish the recruiter had discussed my qualifications with the department representatives BEFORE inviting me in to talk with them."

WINNING MOVES:

In this instance they needed flexibility on both sides, but obviously the hiring manager was not willing to bend. Given that lifetime employment with a single company is no longer the rule, we are beginning to think of employees as "skill sets" that can move from position to position. But most job descriptions still have experience written into them, and it takes some reframing to make that crossover.

WWIII

"I was asked to interview for a project with someone who had a reputation for being difficult to work with. A friend who has worked with her told me something that happened to her on 9/11 when *she* was working on a project for this woman. (Let's call her Sally.)

The building they were in was not far from the Twin Towers. They heard on the news when the Towers collapsed. My friend paused briefly, then went right back to work. Her co-worker couldn't believe it. She asked: '*Why are you still working? This could be the beginning of WWIII?*' My friend replied: '*Because I'm more afraid of Sally than of WWIII.*'

This was at the back of my mind when I made arrangements to fly back east for the interview. It wouldn't have been so bad if the person hadn't changed dates several times after I bought a non-refundable ticket. She apparently had no clue – or didn't care – what it took to plan a short trip whose sole purpose was an interview with her. But the project was a good one, so I persevered. In the end, she offered the job to someone else before I arrived for our meeting. But she still wanted to meet with me, only she wanted to move the time from Monday to Tuesday, the day I was leaving for home. We managed to get together for a short networking meeting before I had to take off, but it was basically a wasted trip."

> **WINNING MOVES:**
> Flexibility doesn't always win the day. But Gumby keeps on smiling.

Free consulting

"It was an exciting opportunity – a large company was creating a new department similar to the one I was currently over. This would be a chance to start afresh and to build everything from the ground up just the way I wanted.

At first it seemed reasonable to me that they were picking my brain for details about my current department. They asked org design questions and wanted to know how I had done this and that and the other thing. They asked about budgets; overcoming internal obstacles; implementation issues; marketing new programs, on and on and on. I got so caught up in the conversation, I didn't immediately notice that they weren't asking any of the usual interview questions.

When I finally asked more about the position, she admitted they had someone internal earmarked for it, but that they had been curious about how other companies went about this type of restructuring. I hadn't been in an actual interview – I had been giving them *free consulting!*"

> **WINNING MOVES:**
> The interviewee was trying to be flexible, but the hiring manager didn't even have enough common sense to keep her hidden agenda out of sight. This is the kind of behavior that gives a company visibility on blogs, and not in a positive light.

It's coming

"It was one of those times when everything seemed to go smoothly. The initial interviews were a success. They liked what I was bringing to the position and weren't at all bothered by a few gaps in my experience for the particular job. They assured me I would pick it up quickly. I survived three hours of psychological testing. I liked the person I would be reporting to. We agreed on general salary and benefits. The contract was being drawn up–.

'It's coming...'

'It's coming...'

'It's coming...'

Over several months, that was the refrain. Then I was told there was a delay because the mayor was reviewing the budget. But it was still 'coming.'

At some point I quit calling them, and they didn't call me. A year later the job was re-posted, and I was still listed as being 'under consideration.' As far as I know, they never hired anyone else. Maybe my contract is lost in some back room at the local post office. Maybe it's still 'coming.' But I'm not holding my breath."

> **WINNING MOVES:**
> Starting dates may be flexible, but they should happen in your lifetime!

Say goodbye to Christmas

"Although I haven't had a disastrous interview per se, I did have a disastrous interview outcome. After going through a series of seven interviews with a health care company, including one with the CEO, I was offered a job. It wasn't my dream job, but it was at a point in my life where I didn't have much money and really needed work. It was right before Christmas, so on the basis of the job offer, I went out and bought a lot of Christmas presents. A lot. When they rescinded the offer (the position went away), I had to return all of them. Not a very merry Christmas."

> **WINNING MOVES:**
> Flexibility should not have to include returning Christmas presents BEFORE Christmas.

Conclusion:

Gumby and his pal Pokey had one adventure after another, always willing to jump in, and never letting anything get them down. Thus the term "Gumbitude," the ultimate in flexibility and resiliency. Many of the interviewees in this chapter had Gumbitude. They ran into obstacles and bounced back. And it's the ability to bounce back that is important. As Mary Pickford explained: *"You may have a fresh start any moment you choose, for this thing that we call 'Failure' is not the falling down, but the staying down."*

LESSONS LEARNED THE EASY WAY
(Through Someone Else's Experience)

Flexibility: Flexibility is usually considered a positive trait, but it doesn't always lead to a successful outcome either during the interview or while waiting on a decision. In addition, one of the challenges in many interviews is coping with the lack of flexibility of the person in charge.

- *If an opportunity presents itself, go for it.*
  Most of us have to pump ourselves up to face stressful situations, so making a decision to take an entirely different direction on the spur of the moment may be difficult. And seizing an opportunity doesn't guarantee success. But it beats kicking yourself afterwards for not giving it a try.

- *Learn from feedback.*
  We know we should learn from feedback, but when it seems like unfair criticism, it isn't easy to be open-minded. And the other person isn't always right. Review, assess, adopt what seems useful, and move on.

- *Know when to let go.*
  We seem to be introduced again and again to evidence that life isn't fair. Pushing back in the moment can be satisfying, but if you are pushing against an inflexible person or position, it may be healthier to simply let your grievance go.

- *Turn flexibility into resiliency.*
  Some people take advantage of the flexibility of others. They may string them along or keep changing the rules because they can get away with it. Flexibility may not result in landing the job, but it gives you the ability to get back up and try something new.

11
You Think Funny

Interview puzzle questions were said to have gone out of vogue a few years ago, but there's a whole mythology about the kinds of questions that have been asked over time to gauge fit, innovation, and the ability to think not only creatively but quickly. For example, Trader Joe's is purported to ask interviewees: *What do you think of garden gnomes?* Assuming they ask this question as a personality test, which of the following responses from an online blog do you think helped the candidate get the job?

- *I prefer gargoyles and dragons instead. Gnomes are too happy.* (dark humor)
- *Gnomes always look happy. They make people smile.* (inane)
- *What value do they offer? And, how does this question relate to the job?* (serious)

Do you want a customer service employee who is quick but says something negative about happiness? Yet, how creative is it to point out that gnomes look happy? And do they really make people smile? Finally, do they want someone with no sense of humor waiting on customers? Even though this appears to be an open-ended question, there is some expectation built in – at least an acknowledgement that the question is offbeat and intended to be fun. So *inane* probably beats *serious* and may be in a dead heat with *dark humor.*

On the other hand Google is said to ask interviewees: *How many people use Facebook in San Francisco at 2:30 pm on a Friday?* If they do ask this question, they are probably less interested in cleverness and more concerned with how the interviewee approaches problem solving.

Several contributors sent me current problem-solution questions they were asked, and one sent a problem solving activity that I've included in this chapter. There are also examples of "trick" questions and one question that only tricked the interviewee. Finally, there's a story about a spur of the moment question that yielded not only some interesting insights into interviewee personalities, but some good party food. Let's begin with the latter.

Better than sex

"Our organization had been undergoing a lot of churn, affecting morale. I was musing about this after one of our potluck farewell lunches. We'd gone from homemade Brie en croute, Chinese chicken salad and bourbon sweet potato pie to store-bought tubs of macaroni salad, microwaved pizza rolls and Costco canisters of red vines.

Mid-musing, I was called into one of our daily group interviews: a semi-circle of eight to twelve managers and employees armed with a printed list of 13 approved questions and two fidgeting candidates. Questioners would take turns running through the list: what are your greatest strengths? Greatest weaknesses? Where do you see yourself in five years? In what areas do you want to grow your skills? Tell us about a time you had to make a tough decision. Responses were fairly typical: team player, I work too hard, in five years I want to be considered a top performer, blah blah blah.

At the end of the approved questions, we were allowed to ask any others we might have. Most of us were anxious to get back to work, but an occasional follow-up question was tossed out. This time, I blurted out, 'What would you bring to a potluck?' My colleagues were not amused, however...

The first candidate (who had professed to being a team player), said, 'I don't do things like that.' So much for team player. The second candidate, who had earlier insisted that she liked to take the initiative and be decisive, replied that she would methodically survey the entire organization (interesting approach) for everyone else's favorite salad. (Will they like me? Am I doing the right thing?) Hmmmm.

I got called in for the next day's interviews and decided to ask the potluck question again. One of the interviewees answered, 'I'd bring my boyfriend.' This was his declaration of being gay (no problem), as well as his assumption that potlucks were open to outsiders (problem). The other person replied, 'I make a killer Better-Than-Sex-Chocolate Fudge cake with a raspberry sauce oozing over the top.' Jaws dropped, faces reddened (we had several prudish managers). The first candidate snorted that rum-cherry sauce would be better. Fudge cake woman quickly became defensive, a deal-breaker for our organization.

Somehow, that potluck question became standard, revealing personality quirks and interpersonal dynamics better than the HR approved ones. Eventually we hired a guy who knew of a local hole-in-the-wall barbecue joint with killer pulled pork - a favorite of our managers. As for me, I would've loved to try anything that was claimed to be better than sex."

> **WINNING MOVES:**
> Since there is no "right" answer to what would you bring to a potluck, this question falls into the "garden gnome" category of culture fit. And since it's a group interview, that adds another interesting dimension - you get to compare answers on the spot. You may not get a knock-your-socks-off response, but you know instantly which candidate's answer — and food - you prefer.

Doing, not telling

"We tried several different approaches with group interviews to see if we could find out more about how a candidate would actually perform on the job. One was the inbox exercise. For this activity, we provided each finalist about 1/2 hour to take up three documents in their 'inbox' and 'handle' them with a written response or directive or next steps in writing. The inbox exercise would include something like this:

'Please call President Sonso regarding his query about the process being used to group purchase new HR software. He feels his institution was not adequately represented in the grading done to review the three bid finalists. Please describe your next steps in handling this potential complaint, particularly with the timeline that has been published and is being followed.'

These responses were then provided to the staff that would be supervised by the chosen candidate for review and comment and joint grading. (FYI, the presidents of each institution participating in the process to choose a new ED also got to review, comment and grade).

As an interviewer, the inbox exercise seemed to me to reveal much more about a person's style, their thinking process, their ability to interact with others, and their (in some cases) scope of knowledge and experience than the more typical approaches. Maybe the fact that they required people to 'do' rather than to 'tell what they do' prevented them from producing the 'comic, tragic and just plain ugly.'"

> **WINNING MOVES:**
> This is similar to the Google question about Facebook and San Francisco in that they wanted to see both the thought process and the outcome. The ability to think and act under pressure is built into the process. And it also gives the candidate some insight into what the organization considers important.

Rent a U-Haul

"A certain large technology company is known for asking complicated problem solving questions to test the creativity, intelligence and thought speed of candidates. The question this particular candidate was asked was: *'How would you move Mt Rainier to Canada?'* He replied: *'Move the boundaries of Canada.'*

The engineering group was both puzzled and surprised by his answer."

> **WINNING MOVES:**
> Perhaps as engineers they were familiar with the "Eleventh Inka" Wayna Qhapaq, imperial leader of the Andean culture in the 1500's that allegedly had unemployed workers move a mountain from one spot to another. Or perhaps they simply wanted calculations – even guesstimates – rather than cleverness.

Shoes, boots and sandals

"A client interviewing for a technical job at a 'very large software firm in the Pacific Northwest' told me about getting the question: *'How many shoes are there in the U.S.?'* He wasn't sure if the question referred only to street shoes so included boots and sandals, just in case."

> **WINNING MOVES:**
> What I like about this question is that you have a chance to come up with a pretty good estimate if you know certain facts, starting with the population of the U.S. On one of the websites about how to answer puzzle questions, they suggest that you ask for any information you need to answer the question. I would add that you should at least lay out your assumptions. This is a good idea when doing any type of real-time problem solving. It's easier to adapt to new information than to just be plain wrong.

Untrained and unskilled

"At one point I was part of a team of untrained interviewers that was assigned the task of interviewing people to fill several similar positions. Although the interviewees might have been surprised by these questions, they were not as surprised by them as I was!

What really 'jazzes' you – you know, what turns you on outside of work?

How do you deal with the fact that I will ask you to do things, like show up to work on time, when I'm not willing to?

When I ask you to do something that is against policy and that might get you fired, how will you go about it?"

WINNING MOVES:

Obviously these were not HR approved questions. I can't help but wonder about the work ethic of the managers who came up with them! Although you can probably learn more from these questions than by asking "If you could be any character on Star Trek, which would you be?" That was an impromptu wild card question that a colleague told me was asked by someone on an interview panel that he sat on. Clever, maybe. Revealing, doubtful. But interviewers I've talked with who ask questions like these tell me they are trying to put the interviewee at ease and lighten things up a bit. Maybe sometimes these questions have the intended impact, although my guess is that they are just as likely to put even more pressure on the candidate. Now they not only have to be lucid and insightful but clever.

I speak Latin

"I was fresh out of college and saw a computer-related job advertised in the newspaper. I applied and got an interview. During the interview I was asked: *What languages do you know?* I replied that I knew Latin and Spanish. Only afterwards did I realize they were referring to computer languages!

Needless to say, I did not get the job."

WINNING MOVES:

Res ipsa loquitur. (The thing speaks for itself.)

I'm scared!

"Sometimes the stories people tell each other about interview experiences make you really wonder about what goes through the minds of the interviewers. A friend of mine interviewed for a position at a large, global organization. She had a full day of interviews and with each successive person was asked, '*What scares you about this position in this organization?*' After a while she began to sense that this was a trick question. Was there a right answer? Would they compare all of her answers to see if she was consistent? Was this THE question that would determine whether she was hired or not?

At the end of the day she met with her seventh interviewer and was asked the same question: '*What scares you about working in this position in this organization?*' This time she responded that what scared her was that everyone she had met during the course of the day had asked her this question.

She was not offered the position. Maybe she wasn't scared enough."

WINNING MOVES:
I think I would rather be asked: Why are there interstate highways in Hawaii?

Conclusion:

Pop psychology and action questions can be fun and may even provide insights into the creativity, problem solving, and personality of the candidate. I talked to one person who actually wanted to interview with a company that asked offbeat questions simply for the challenge. But for many, knowing that your chances of getting a job you want may depend on how you respond to something you've never given any thought to can be an unnerving experience.

In his book, *Kitchen Confidential*, author and chef Anthony Bourdain tells the story of an interview he had with the owner of a high-end chain of steak houses. The interviewer had a thick brogue, and Bourdain was having difficulty understanding the questions posed to him. It got to the point where he felt uncomfortable asking the interviewer to repeat the question. So when he was asked something that struck him as a bit odd, he didn't hesitate to respond to what he thought he heard: *'What do you know about me?'* He replied: *'Absolutely nothing.'* It would have increased his chances of landing the job if he had heard the last word as 'meat' rather than 'me.'

The key to answering a question, any type of question, is to first make sure you know *what* was asked, and, in the case of a trick question, it's helpful to also know *why* it was asked. But in the moment, you can only guess. Is it to test whether you have a sense of humor? How you process problems? How you handle pressure? Your ability to think on your feet? Maybe they just want to know if they can improve the quality of their potlucks by hiring you. Give it your best shot and then quit worrying about what you should have said when they asked: *"If nothing ever sticks to a Teflon pan, then how do they make Teflon stick to the pan?"* So you talked about how Teflon was originally made with polymers and chains of fluorine atoms and additives but now they have a new smooth process using sticky molecules… and they were hoping for a humorous response. You didn't really want that job anyway.

LESSONS LEARNED THE EASY WAY
(Through Someone Else's Experience)

Questions: Not knowing what questions you will be asked in an interview is one of the main causes of stress. Making sure you know *what* was asked and perhaps the *reason* it was asked can help you come up with a relevant and satisfactory answer.

- *If you don't have a witty answer for an off-the-wall question, fall back on process.* If you are given a question that calls for instant creativity and nothing comes to mind, don't despair. Lay out your assumptions and what you would need to know in order to give a complete answer. In other words, show your thought process. In the end, that may be as effective as a snappy response.

- *Don't panic.*
  If you are given an assignment to do something in a short period of time, quickly assess how much you can prepare in the time allotted and proceed accordingly. They don't expect perfection; they want to know how you approach getting things done. You can even include a list of tasks/questions that you would pursue if given more time. The key is to be realistic and not panic. Did I mention taking a deep breath before beginning?

- *Don't read too much into a question.*
  Not every set of interview questions gets the rigorous vetting it should. Sometimes unclear or silly questions get asked. If you are unlucky enough to get one of those, make the best of it. You can rephrase if it's too unclear. "If what you mean by _____ is_____, then..." If it's a frivolous question, you can treat it with a light-hearted response. Just don't get bogged down in trying to give a thorough response to a bad question.

12
Spinach in Your Teeth

There is a story about a Russian cosmonaut on a solo mission who hears a constant tapping sound in the control panel of his spacecraft. Tap, tap, tap. After a while, it starts to drive him mad. He rips out the controls and searches everywhere, but he can't find the source. The tapping becomes torture. Finally, he decides he must fall in love with this sound instead of hating it. He starts to hum a tune in time with the tapping. The sound disappears, replaced by music. And he is once again able to concentrate.

Although researchers vary in their findings on the length of an average adult's attention span these days, most agree that attention spans are decreasing due to technology and multi-tasking. For example, it is estimated that most internet users spend less than one minute on the average website, and some employees are said to check their email as many as 30-40 times an hour. Not only do we focus less, we are easily distracted.

"I don't have a short attention span, I just... Oh, look a squirrel!"

"I'd have a longer attention span if so many things weren't so shiny!"

We may not be alone in a spacecraft with a tapping sound that won't stop, but there are plenty of other obstacles to concentration in our environment. And sometimes they find their way into an interview.

One person who has a story represented elsewhere in this book, told me about an interview he went on sporting a large stain on the front of his shirt. That was the only thing he remembered about the interview. But he said it reminded him of a 2008 Procter and Gamble commercial in which a Talking Stain would yell gibberish each time the interviewee spoke, totally distracting the interviewer. The commercial was an advertisement for the Tide-to-Go pen. The message: remove stains before they out talk you. There are no talking stains in the following stories. Instead, flies of one kind or another figure prominently in the first three stories, and the women in the remaining stories have their own share of wardrobe issues to contend with.

One fly or two?

"The candidate had already been prescreened. Since he lived in another city that was easy to get to by a short plane ride, my boss and I decided to take the plane there, interview the candidate in the airport, and fly home.

Unfortunately, when we got there, we faced a number of problems. The only place to meet was in an open, noisy café that was littered with food from the lunch crowd. And, it was hot, very HOT. But we found a table and took out our interview questions.

The candidate was a bit late, so by the time he arrived, there was a lot of sweating going on. Both my boss and the candidate had slightly receding hairlines, and I noticed beads of sweat gathering on their foreheads. Then it happened. We were just beginning the interview when I saw a lone fly circling and coming our way. It seemed to take place in slow motion, the interview questions and the circling fly, two story lines destined to meet.

Its target was our candidate's forehead and the beads of sweat that glistened like runway lights. At first the candidate tried to ignore the fly, but as it kept on circling, looking for a safe place to land, he tried to discretely brush it away. The fly was persistent though. It tried again, and again, and again. I wasn't counting, but I think it made at least 10-15 attempts to touch down on the sweat beads. 'Trying to anticipate what the fly was going to do next' became almost secondary to the interview questions.

Finally I couldn't stand it anymore. I said, 'Would you like to take care of that fly before we continue?' The candidate stopped in mid-sentence; no one said anything. I suddenly realized that he thought I had said 'take care of YOUR fly,' and that in his mind he wasn't sure if he had one or two flies to deal with – the one buzzing around his head and the other one 'open.'

After we re-grouped, it took about two minutes for the three of us to kill the fly before continuing with the interview. The ending may not have been good for the fly, but it was for the candidate - he got the job."

> **WINNING MOVES:**
> "Flight of the Bumblebee" is an orchestral piece that most of us associate with popular frenetic renditions of the original. Not the slow motion approach of the fly in this story. But both share a mesmerizing inevitability as the denouement draws near. Kudos to the three people involved for making the best of a situation filled with distractions. This story is a good example of why you sometimes need to call attention to what's really going on instead of hoping it will go away.

Wardrobe malfunction

"When we hire adjunct faculty, we have a two-step interview. The first is just an informal get-to-know-the applicant and then, if we think the person exhibits good communication skills, we follow that interview with another session in which we have a detailed discussion about the position.

For one of the first-session interviews, our interviewing room was being used by someone else, so we assembled in the lounge area of our building. There are no tables there, so we just arranged some chairs in a circle so the four of us could talk with the interviewee in an informal setting.

We brought the interviewee into the room and, in our circle facing each other, talked with him for 15 to 20 minutes. All of us were clearly distracted, fidgeting, looking at each other periodically, and smiling at each other. We politely ended the interview, thanked the applicant for meeting with us, and escorted him out of the room. When the interview team returned to the lounge to discuss the interview, we all burst into laughter. The applicant had gone through the entire interview with his trouser fly not only in the *down* position, but in a *very* open position. We did not invite the candidate back to a second interview phase, but he made a very memorable impression, not necessarily positive, on all of us."

WINNING MOVES:

When it happens to Justin Bieber they call it a wardrobe malfunction. And whether at the Grammy's or at the Liverpool Echo Arena (yes, he's had the problem at least twice in the last year), his fans don't care.

Unfortunately, in this interview, the candidate would have been better off if there had been flies buzzing around his head – they might at least have distracted the interviewers from noticing the problem with the other fly.

Did the interviewers do the right thing in failing to call attention to the problem? My guess is that they felt it was more embarrassing to say something than to appear to ignore the gap. Of course, afterwards, the candidate surely noticed. Is there anything he could have said in a thank you note to mitigate this image? I doubt it. In this case, I think the fly wins and everyone else loses.

Ziippp

"You always replay events you would like to change in your mind. Over and over. *What if–. If I had only–.* Over and over. When all I would really like to do is forget it ever happened. Not that it changed my life or hangs over me like a dark cloud. I didn't know any of the people who witnessed the event before it happened, and I haven't seen any of them since. But I wish it had never happened.

Yes, it was the cliché 'your zipper is open' situation. I was seated in a chair in front of a panel of interviewers. They had a table to hide behind; I didn't. If I hadn't been running late and needed to change clothes in the car, it wouldn't have happened. But I had and it did. Leaning forward with my legs apart, I enthusiastically responded to a question asked. It was about ten minutes into the interview. I'm not sure what made me look down, but I did. It wasn't just a tiny opening but a huge gap with underwear clearly visible.

'Sorry,' I said as I zipped up. Once I noticed what else could I do?

Somehow I completed the interview, but I wasn't surprised not to get the job. It had been a longshot anyway. But sometimes I think about the conversation that must have taken place after I left. Did they laugh? Feel sorry for me? Respect my decision to zip up? Wonder why I didn't just leave? And why didn't someone on the panel ask for a short break and let me know what was going on? I'll never know the answer to any of these questions. And that's okay – after this, I'm going to pretend it never happened."

WINNING MOVES:
Ten minutes into an interview and you discover your fly is open. You have a couple of options; but leaving it open isn't one of them. When it happens to someone else, it's funny. When it happens to you, it's tragic. The good news is that he didn't make the headlines (*Zip it up, Justin!*), and no pictures were posted online.

You have a ...

"The candidate was very capable and presented well; however, it was difficult to look past the curler she had forgotten in her hair."

WINNING MOVES:
Number 1: Didn't she comb her hair or look in the mirror before the interview?!
Number 2: What color was the curler? (Tell me it wasn't hot pink–)
Number 3: Didn't she comb her hair or look in the mirror before the interview?!?!
Obviously the "winning move" in this instance would have been to look at yourself before going in for the interview.

Please take it off

"A very awkward seeming woman came in for an interview for an administrative position. She was dressed in business casual, with a 1950's look, like an extra from *Mad Men*, but not pretty. She had her purse on her shoulder. It wasn't a purse with a long shoulder strap, but a short shoulder bag. She looked like she was ready to make a run for it at a moment's notice.

Overall, her awkwardness told us more about her than our questions and answers. She did not get the position.

Afterwards she asked for feedback, and the interviewer she talked with was honest with her. She explained how distracting the purse with the short strap had been for everyone, but she couldn't tell by the woman's response – or lack of response - if she understood that the purse had set a tone for the entire interview. We'll never know for sure. The series was renewed, but the woman with the purse wasn't a continuing character."

WINNING MOVES:
In the 1950s workers were more formal, said to be more committed to their jobs, and often stayed with a company their entire career. Maybe this candidate was making a statement that the interviewers missed. On the other hand, maybe she just likes vintage clothes.

Peekaboo

"As I was getting on the elevator after an interview with a middle-aged, very attentive male, I was thinking about how well it had gone. Then I caught my reflection in the mirrored wall and realized that I'd popped a button on my shirt – the one right between my boobs. Hmmm, I thought, yep, I'll probably get that one. And I did."

WINNING MOVES:
In this instance was a show of cleavage a distraction or a deal maker? Hard to know–.

Run!

"The interview was for a school district assistant superintendent position and was being held in a public forum of about 50 people. It was the end of the day. When the interviewee came in she seemed confident and energetic. Only later did I reflect on how she must have been feeling with the gigantic run in her stocking.

'*I want to say something right up front*,' she announced at the beginning of her interview. She went on to explain how earlier in the day she had snagged her nylon on something, hence the stripe down her leg that was very visible to all. Once she got that out of the way, she went on to give an excellent interview. In some ways, it was how she handled the run in her nylon that made the biggest impression."

WINNING MOVES:
Talk about turning lemons into lemonade! It's good to know that sometimes a distraction can be addressed in a positive manner and the interview move on to more serious issues.

Conclusion:

Whether the story about the Russian Cosmonaut is just a fable or really happened doesn't matter. We all want to think that we can ignore the tapping or the "spinach in the teeth" and give someone a fair hearing. But when something strange or bizarre happens, it's human nature to find our eyes drawn to the very thing we don't want to look at. It's worthwhile to note, however, that at least three of the individuals from these stories actually got hired in spite of (or because of) what happened to them. So there is hope. Just check the mirror before you go in for your interview, a full-length mirror.

LESSONS LEARNED THE EASY WAY
(Through Someone Else's Experience)

Distractions: The message about distractions is two-fold – don't get distracted, and don't *be* the distraction.

- *For men, check your fly before going into the interview.*
  An interview takes you outside of your routine. That's the reason there are so many stories about someone whose fly was open. To be safe, do a last-minute check.

- *Call out distractions.*
  If there is something happening (like a fly buzzing around) that everyone is aware of, you are better off to acknowledge what is going on rather than trying to ignore it. The harder you try to ignore something, the more distracting it becomes. And that is probably true for everyone in the room.

- *Pay attention to nonverbals.*
  If someone seems to be staring at you - or the opposite, someone avoiding looking at you - there may be a reason. Do a mental check of the possibilities: unbuttoned blouse, curler in your hair, spinach on a front tooth, a tag hanging from a jacket, a bug crawling up your sleeve (yes, this happened in a meeting to someone I know), whatever. If you can figure it out on your own, correct the problem. Whether or not you say something as you make the correction depends on the situation. If you are certain something isn't right and you can't figure it out, you may want to ask. Although if they haven't already said something about what's distracting them, it might be an uncomfortable exchange. In the end, I think it's better to be told you have a curler in your hair than to find out after the fact.

13
Let's Get Engaged

A recent Society for Human Resource Management (SHRM) survey found that four out of five U.S. employees surveyed said they were satisfied with their jobs. Yet most research suggests that over half of all employees are not engaged in their work. Satisfied but not engaged? That sounds like quite a few people are putting in their time while perhaps still hoping to find that dream job. But even if they aren't engaged in the workplace, surely they put on their enthusiastic, I'm engaged hat during an interview. Surprisingly, some of the following stories would suggest otherwise.

On a scale of 1-10, with one low and ten high, the first three stories don't raise the enthusiasm meter needle enough to have it register on the chart! Next there are several stories that demonstrate different ways to relate lack of engagement. Finally, the last two stories show how important a perceived passion for the job can be to those in a position to make an offer.

Apathy Department

"Three of us were interviewing applicants for a customer service manager position in state government. Several of the questions we use are meant to learn what impressions a candidate has of her own contribution, strengths and weaknesses, etc. One candidate, a slightly built woman dressed in muted grays and browns, timidly took the 'seat' to have her moment under the bright lights of the interview.

When the candidate was asked '*What would your co-workers say is your greatest strength?*' her deadpan answer was '*my sense of humor.*' We looked at each other and wondered if it could possibly be true. Several questions later, I asked the candidate what she believed was her greatest contribution to the work group. She answered '*apathy.*' Incredulous, I asked her to please repeat her answer. She replied: '*Apathy is a word.*' I immediately replied, '*Yes, but it's the wrong word.*' I got kicked under the table on that one.

She did not get the job, but we considered establishing an apathy department where everyone is fully engaged with the mission of the organization. No slackers allowed."

WINNING MOVES:

Just to be sure I checked out definitions of apathy. They all agreed on some version of lack of interest or emotion. And there are no synonyms that are in any way flattering. So it remains a puzzle as to why she chose that particular word to characterize her contribution to her team unless none of the interviewers recognized her deadpan or dry humor for what it was.

What is dry humor? It's the humor minus the saliva.

Very dynamic

"I was looking for an experienced trainer, and, on paper, this individual looked pretty good. However, during the interview she came across very flat, not a desirable quality for a trainer who has to hold the attention of participants. Nor did her answers to my questions suggest that she had the necessary experience for the job. As the interview evolved, she became more and more morose and I was concluding that she was not the right person for the job. Still, it seemed only fair to give her one last opportunity to save face and end the interview on a positive note.

'*Would the participants in your workshops characterize you as dynamic?*' I prompted. Being dynamic is a key quality for a trainer, and sometimes people are different in front of a group than they are in one-on-one situations. But, instead of responding to my cue to toot her own horn and project a little energy, she lowered her head, and in a very quiet voice replied, '*Yes, I am very dynamic.*'"

WINNING MOVES:

Another example of dry humor? Or—dynamic compared to what?

The world "inexplicable" comes to mind. It's like someone applying for a position in finance and describing themselves as "not a numbers person."

Contact your inner self

"There are usually expectations about what the interview will be like based on the position you are applying for. So when I landed an interview with a director of OD (organizational development), and he appeared to be a cold fish, I was surprised. He seemed very distant and impersonal, shared no information about himself, and didn't seem particularly interested in any personal information about me. He simply went methodically through his list of questions, leaving no time for me to ask anything. I kept thinking, 'THIS is the director of OD?!'

After persevering through four more interviews with different configurations of teams with similar behavior patterns, I was offered the job. So I called out this behavior as a potential problem in how we would work together. The OD director responded by saying they were intentionally trying to be non-reactive, and, when asked something that elicited any sort of emotional reaction in them, they would go inside, become aware of their feelings and respond from a calm, centered, and grounded place similar to a person meditating. Although I had some doubts about the desirability of the approach, I accepted the position.

It is still to be determined how my career will turn out at this new organization. Perhaps I need to meditate on it."

WINNING MOVES:

This is an interesting approach to leveling the playing field for the interview process. I assume that they didn't ask any oddball questions like *What kind of ice cream flavor would you be?* Or, *On a scale of 1-5, how weird are you?* To many interviewees these are emotionally challenging questions. Imagine what it would be like providing a clever answer to deadpan stares. Not sure I care much for this technique, but it would be interesting to find out how the interviewers felt about the results.

That famous coffee place

"I was invited for a day of interviews and was looking forward to seeing inside the HQ of an international coffee chain. The people were very friendly, and the interviews seemed to be progressing well - despite (surprisingly) not being offered a cup of coffee!

At the 3rd interview, which was with a team of people, one of the interviewers looked at me with a coffee in her hand and asked, '*Have you had a coffee?*' to which I replied, '*No, no one has offered one.*' She looked quite horrified and without thinking about the impact of what I was about to say, I added, '*Don't worry, up until you introduced Pike Place I didn't like your coffee.*' Not a sensible thing to say where the love of their coffee is more than a religion!

Needless to say I did not get the job."

WINNING MOVES:

This story could have been in the chapter on honesty or the one on missteps, but I included it here because it illustrates the level of commitment required of employees in some companies for the product they produce. I remember someone telling me that she was hesitant to apply to a company that sold sporting goods because she wasn't athletic. But she really liked the job description. On the other hand, when I worked at Boeing, I was amazed that no matter what function the employee supported, they always said their job was to "build airplanes." Most people "get" what it takes to be engaged. It's just surprising how few say they are when asked on an internal company survey.

Beam me up, Scotty

"I had been invited to apply for a job that I wasn't entirely sure I wanted. But it was a high-level, good position that would pay well, so I agreed to the interview. One of the things I didn't like about it was that the offices were located in a small city on the outskirts of the larger city where I currently worked and lived.

On the day of the interview, I got dressed up in my best suit and was ready to give it a shot. So I started driving in what I assumed to be the right direction. When I didn't end up where I thought I should be, I pulled over and looked at my map. I drove some more. I found the street listed on the instructions, but it was blocked by major construction. I called the interview office and explained that I was lost. They said I wasn't far and gave me directions. I drove some more. The second time I called the same receptionist for help I was well over an hour late. After some more wandering around, I just could not face calling her again.

Strangely enough, once I turned around I had no trouble finding my way home."

> **WINNING MOVES:**
> "Beam me up, Scotty," the famous phrase from Star Trek that was never actually said on the series, has become synonymous with being instantly transported from one place to another. Today, we can instruct our GPS to "transport" us somewhere, although we have to do most of the work ourselves. Still, it's much easier to find a location with GPS than with a map. Of course even maps get you where you want to go, assuming you really do want to reach your destination. Sometimes your inner voice is the best navigation system.

Should I whinny?

"I asked a friend for an introduction to a well-known organization that she is associated with and got a quick response. But the meeting was scheduled a long way out. When the day came I was met by two people. One was a bubbly, personable woman who seemed to find everything hilarious. As we walked to the meeting room she pointed out her favorite artwork and at one point picked up a puppet and started goofing off. The other woman just looked tired, very tired.

As the conversation began, the tired woman began to yawn loudly. Things just got better when each time she asked me a question, her eyelids and chin would start to droop as I responded. At one point I said, 'You look so tired. I wish I could get you a cup of coffee.' Instead of acknowledging that she was nodding off as I spoke, she just said that she had not got enough sleep the night before. I joked and told her that I felt like I was talking fast because she seemed so tired. That got no response.

Finally, I tried to check their understanding of the purpose of the meeting and was told that they were trying to add to their 'stable of consultants.' But it didn't feel like I was the 'horse' they were looking for.

The bubbly woman's initially welcoming 'hilarity' gradually became inside jokes, which I was clearly on the outside of. At times the conversation was almost combative. For example, they described their org chart and said that it would look like the people at the top make decisions but actually there were a lot of people in the middle with more seniority. I said that sometimes that's good. They disagreed. When I paralleled my work with another organization with theirs, the response was, 'No, we aren't like them.' My description of a highly successful project with a past client was met with, 'That wouldn't work here.'

At one point during the interview, the sleepy woman turned to her colleague and sighed, 'You've been out of the country, but I have had *hundreds* of these interviews.'

I'm not sure how many consultants fit in a stable, but this pony says *neeeeighhhh*."

WINNING MOVES:

You can't get any more disengaged than to fall asleep while someone is talking. Although unnecessary disagreement runs a close second. Sometimes interviewers act as though they are behind a one-way mirror instead of actually IN the room with the interviewee. It is best to remember how small the world can be. You never know when the person you insult today will be in a position to make a difference in your life tomorrow.

Eagle Scout

"I was twenty-five, had two kids, had just finished graduate school, and was unemployed. I needed a job! And my resume was skimpy to say the least. I'd only had teen and college jobs. I'd even listed 'Eagle Scout' as one of my credentials. So when I got an interview at a start-up company, I was determined to put my best foot forward.

The recruiter was supposed to hire people to staff a new office in just two days. It was a wireless company that was expanding and was on a short deadline to put some towers up. She didn't spend more than about fifteen minutes with me, but she told me that she loved my 'energy' and my 'positive attitude.' And she was impressed that I had been an Eagle Scout. Then she offered me the job.

When I arrived for my first day of work, I didn't even have a computer or a telephone – both had been ordered but weren't available yet. I did, however, have a desk and a chair, and they found a mobile phone for me to use. It was not, however, entirely clear what they wanted me to do.

Meanwhile, I had an interview at another, well-established company. The interviewer and I hit it off, but he acknowledged that I needed experience. *'Let's get you some experience,'* he said when he offered me the job. So after only two weeks, I left the start-up for the other position."

WINNING MOVES:

Most of us start new jobs hoping for and perhaps even expecting the best. But it doesn't take much to start seeing the cup as half empty rather than at least half full. And even an Eagle Scout can let you down when faced with a better deal.

Sausage and eggs

"We were hiring a Training Specialist, and I got the joy of doing a phone interview with every internal applicant whether they were qualified or not. I dutifully scheduled all phone calls in advance and asked which number would be best to call.

One applicant I called was at home since it was her day off. She informed me that she was cooking breakfast as we conducted the interview. She told me up front, *'Since it's my day off, I'm cooking a late breakfast of eggs, hash browns and sausage.'* So she cooked and answered questions...not too many though. Regardless of her multi-tasking she didn't meet the qualifications.

And, yes, she was bummed when I informed her we wouldn't be moving forward in the process with her.

I wonder if it was a tasty breakfast?"

WINNING MOVES:

Years ago, I remember a friend telling me about an interview where she went in and the hiring manager was on the computer but told her to go ahead and talk about her qualifications; she was able to multi-task. My recollection is that the hiring manager also took a telephone call during the interview. My friend did not get the job, and actually didn't want it by the end of the conversation. If you aren't important enough to get the other person's sole attention during an interview, what would it be like to work for them?

The same holds true for the woman making breakfast. Maybe multi-tasking is one of her core competencies, but you have to wonder about her ability to focus.

Cautionary tale

"As a consultant you hear all sorts of stories from clients. One that I remember was about an interview a client would never forget, a sort of cautionary tale.

The interview had gone well and he was offered the job. They even discussed salary and the comp plan. It seemed like a done deal. But, being on the cautious side, my client indicated that he wanted to think about it and talk it over with his spouse. He asked if he could get back to the prospective employer the next day, and they said 'yes.'

The next day when he called to accept the offer, he was told that the job offer had been withdrawn because he didn't seem that excited about the position or the organization."

WINNING MOVES:

Most people probably feel like this candidate should have been informed that he needed to make a decision on the spot if they were going to reject him for not doing so. On the other hand, the prospective employer may have reacted with what Daniel Kahneman has labeled "fast thinking" by believing there was some narrative coherence in the way the candidate conducted himself during the interview combined with asking for time to think before accepting the position. Put simply, they wanted someone excited about the job and had a case of buyer's remorse when they were put on hold. Was the decision logical? Perhaps not. But hiring decisions are often based as much on feeling as on logic. In this instance it was just more obvious.

West of Mississippi

"It was my first formal career interview after graduation. I was excited and open to possibilities. So when they asked me where I wanted to be located, I said, 'The Pacific Northwest, California, or any place west of Mississippi.'

I'm not sure if the answer seemed a bit desperate or just eager, but shortly after that I was flown to Seattle for an interview. I had never been there before. After meeting with the hiring manager, I spent the rest of the day in a meet-and-greet before flying home. I was too new to the process to ask what would be happening next.

When the recruiter called me and asked *'What did you think?'* I talked on and on and on, waiting for a job offer. When it didn't come, I finally had the sense to ask the right question. He was apparently waiting for me to demonstrate interest and be direct about wanting the job. I almost missed my chance!

That was on Friday. By Monday I was in Kalamazoo at management boot camp."

WINNING MOVES:

In sales training they instruct you on when and how to make "the ask." This is the pivotal moment in the relationship between buyer and seller. Or between a candidate and a prospective employer. "You have a job; I want it." Many see the interview process as a more indirect exchange with the prospective employer in control. But how is that employer supposed to gauge your level of interest at the end of the interview if you don't tell them? A confirmation that you want the job cannot do any harm and just may cinch the deal.

Conclusion:

Most experts on finding a job in the current market encourage applicants to research the companies they apply to. You can then adapt your resume to the specific position and, if you get an interview, you can talk intelligently about what they do in relationship to your skills and experience. Although realistically no one expects someone looking for a job to apply for their first choice and then just wait to see if they get it before applying for anything else, each prospective employer wants to feel as though they are number one. They expect candidates to be enthusiastic not only about the position, but about the organization. If someone fails to demonstrate engagement *during* the interview, how can anyone expect them to be engaged when faced with day-to-day challenges on the job?

LESSONS LEARNED THE EASY WAY
(Through Someone Else's Experience)

Enthusiasm: If you don't express some enthusiasm for the job during the interview, it's unlikely the interviewer(s) will be excited about you as a candidate.

- *Monitor your energy level.*
  Try to be aware of how you are coming across. Nervousness often manifests itself in either hyperactivity or in low energy. If you find yourself leaning across the table or tapping a pen, back off and put the pen down. If your shoulders are slumped and your voice weak, sit up straight and try to project. These are obvious examples. What you actually do may be more subtle. But the goal is to be appropriately enthusiastic during the interview, nothing more nor less.

- *Don't necessarily take your energy level cues from the interviewer(s).*
  Your interviewer(s) may feel like their role is to ask the questions and assess your response, not engage you in conversation. That may not be the best interview technique, but there are some hiring managers who feel this way. Or they may simply be so focused on the assessment that they don't think about the impact of their energy level on yours. Remember: you are the one in the spotlight.

- *Know what excites your interviewer(s) about their company, and show them you care.*
  You are expected to know what the company stands for, at least in a general way, before the interview. Let the interviewer(s) know that you are excited about their organization and its mission/products/ services by what you say as well as by your tone and demeanor.

- *Be realistic about the level of enthusiasm displayed by the interviewer(s).*
  It can be difficult to assess whether those interviewing you really want to hire you or if they will support you once you are in the position. Pay attention to any red flags. If they don't seem particularly interested in what you have to say during the interview, it's doubtful they will change their tune once you are on board. It's much easier to say "no" to a job offer than to leave soon after taking a job.

- *Let them know that you want the job.*
  Applying for a position isn't the equivalent of publicly declaring your interest. At the end of the interview, not only thank them for their time, tell them that you are even more excited about the position now that you've talked with them. We all like to feel that what we have to offer is something special.

14
The OMG Index

Southwest Airlines popularized the group interview in which groups of applicants are brought in together to interact with interviewers and each other. The goal is to see how people deal with each other and determine culture fit. Some version of the group interview has become an accepted and frequent part of the interview process, but there's a lot of variation of structure and results.

OMG or digispeak, otherwise known as IMglish, is used to express extreme incredulity about something. In the interview world, it is often used to describe how interviewees feel about the group interview: "OMG, you won't believe what happened at my interview!" The approach brings to mind the reality television show *Survivor* in which contestants compete against each other and can also be "voted off the island" by other contestants. Although candidates in a group interview can't vote each other out of the running for the job, they often try to one-up each other in order to "win" the competition. However, the ultimate power to determine the "Sole Survivor" is in the hands of the group conducting the interview.

The first story in this chapter is the group interview as told from the interviewer's perspective, and the second from an observer's point of view. Several other iterations of the group interview are told from the interviewee's point of view, including experiences with the panel interview and group competition interviews in which each candidate is given the same task and then evaluated against each other. OMG!

Raising the interview bar

"Most of the interviews I've participated in have seemed more 'beige' than comic or tragic. Everyone is on good behavior. What I would like to share is an interview process in which I was part of a group of interviewers. Although the approach did not produce any *tragic* or particularly *humorous* interviews, I found it to be far more interesting and revealing than the standard interview.

We conducted a group interview with recreation supervisors - all of whom had openings for a recreation center director (3 to be exact). We had between 8 - 10 finalists; and we invited them all in for a large group session. We had about 5 questions on a sheet of paper which had this style to it:

'Your center serves a diverse demographic including blacks, immigrants from Vietnam and Cambodia with little English, and whites. How will you go about determining programs for these populations? Discuss with others in this group as if you were all staffing this center.'

The instructions were to get underway without initiation by any of the other interviewers and give each question 10 - 15 minutes for discussion.

In these leaderless group interviews, we rather more enjoyed those people who used some self-deprecating remarks to put themselves and the others at ease and especially people who listened, confirmed agreement with good ideas, and used summation before presenting their own ideas or synthesis of others' ideas. And most particularly, we appreciated those that did not try to dominate or take center stage."

> **WINNING MOVES:**
> From the comments made about the preferences of the interviewers, it sounds like the group of candidates handled the situation professionally and that culture fit was fairly easy to determine through observation of the process.

In general, most interviews like this evaluate candidates on their ability to lead, listen, and pull ideas together. Given the short amount of time usually allotted for this type of exercise, the more vocal participants tend to push things along to reach resolution. Paying attention to interpersonal communication while at the same time working to achieve a result may be tricky for the interviewees, yet that may just be what the interviewers are watching for. At the same time it makes you wonder WWOD? (What would Oprah do?)

Who was that lady?!

"Once upon a time, I was a new supervisor who didn't know much about conducting an interview. So I asked a colleague who had an interview scheduled with a candidate if I could sit in and observe. He agreed, and so I joined him, another interviewer and the candidate in a very small office just as the interview was starting. Since there were four of us in a very tight space, I ended up sitting in a corner behind the candidate. For the entire interview I was looking at the back of his head.

At the end of the interview when the candidate was asked if he had any questions, he said: *'Just one - who is that lady sitting behind me?'*"

WINNING MOVES:

From the front of the room it must have looked a little like the Vice President or Speaker of the House sitting behind the President. Definitely not BSA (best seat available).

Obviously, the candidate should be told who the people in the room are. But it's easy to overlook this kind of detail when the setting is less than optimal. Unfortunately, it's hard to know how much impact the setting had on the performance of the candidate.

A better paper airplane

"I was not told that it was going to be a group interview, so I was surprised that there were five other people being interviewed with me. The interviewers started by watching us participate in an ice breaker – the one where you have a name on a piece of paper attached to the back of your head and you try to guess the who you are based on the yes-no questions we were asked. That was okay, but I didn't know what it proved. Then we took a quiz. It also didn't seem to make much sense given the job we were all vying for.

The highlight was when each of us had to make a presentation on how to build a paper airplane. Fortunately I knew how, and I enjoy making presentations, but there was at least one person who didn't have a clue. Again, if we had been applying for a job building paper airplanes or making stuff up in the moment, all this would have made sense. But it was fun.

Finally, we were asked to take a psychological exam. Then we were told that we would be called back if we were a good fit. I'm not sure if I should be more pleased by not being called back–."

> **WINNING MOVES:**
> Sometimes it's difficult to know what the group interview is intended to reveal. Hopefully this group had something very specific in mind even if they did not reveal it to their candidates. Maybe the company was planning on entering a paper airplane contest and needed talented yet mentally stable participants–. HHOK (ha, ha, only kidding).

Back on the playground

"I have a client who shared a terrible interview experience with me. She was told to be prepared for a group interview. She (and I) thought this would mean a panel interview or an interview with an entire department etc. However, the interview took place in a large room with a group of applicants all vying for attention and the opportunity to give the correct answer in front of each other. Bedlam ensued and my client was exasperated."

> **WINNING MOVES:**
> Trying to see how people respond under stress? Looking for a dominant, competitive individual? Or just feeling mean that day–? DQMOT (don't quote me on this).
>
> One story I remember from an HR colleague is a group interview in which one of the candidates kept saying, "What he said," when asked a question. The "he" was another candidate.

Krispy Kreme, anyone?

"I was interviewing before a panel to move from a regional to a headquarters position in organizational effectiveness. They went through the normal rotation of questions process, and I felt like I was doing well. Then they introduced the 'situation' challenge based on getting an already high performing team to the next level of performance. I was to address the problem from both a theoretical and a practical perspective. Not only was I to come up with a recommendation and explain the 'why,' but I was also supposed to tell them what I *considered* recommending and what I decided to leave out...and why. They gave me a flip chart, some pens, and about 20-30 minutes to prepare.

Left alone to work on my presentation, I felt like tossing a pen in the air and walking out. But under the circumstances, I didn't think I could do that. So I took a deep breath and started writing.

A few minutes later one of the interviewers came back into the room and started talking about the new Krispy Kreme store that had opened up in the area. She told me that she had some coupons she couldn't use and offered one to me. I thanked her and declined.

Then two more of the interviewers came back into the room. They proceeded to chit chat about this and that as well as about one of the other candidates – my competition. Needless to say, it was difficult to concentrate on the task at hand.

Finally I made my pitch. That got me an interview with the Director for final approval. And I was offered the job.

After I was there awhile and realized that the interview questions and process had been put together by the I/O group (Industrial Organizational Psychologists), I became suspicious about my experience. Perhaps they had planned the interruptions to see whether I could be easily distracted or to test my people versus task focus. (Or to see whether I liked Krispy Kreme donuts.) It made sense. So I asked.

Although they wished it had been a deliberate ploy, apparently what happened was purely coincidental. The Krispy Kreme offer had been legitimate. But they decided it was a good idea to add 'distractions' as part of the interview process."

> **WINNING MOVES:**
> She passed a separate test by being able to stay focused despite interruptions, and didn't even get credit for that. @TETD (at the end of the day) the important thing was getting the job.

Goldilocks and the three choices

"My interview had been going well. There was only one more hurdle – a 15 minute presentation with follow-up questions. They gave me three topics to choose from and 35 minutes to prepare. But there were a few caveats: I couldn't use my iPad or cell during the prep, and I could only use flipcharts for the presentation. It seemed a bit primitive, but that was fine. I'm comfortable making presentations and used to adapting to different situations.

The topic options reminded me of Goldilocks and the three bowls of porridge. The first was a lukewarm choice. Most people in the profession would say about the same thing, and the interviewers might be less than enthusiastic about either the tried-and-true or an extremely unusual approach. The second was a virtual landmine, more their field of expertise than mine, and I had no idea what their specific views were on the topic. But the third option seemed just right - using a book I had read recently to discuss my views on management and leadership development.

Fortunately, I am a reader, and I had quite a few books to choose from. But I wanted to be creative rather than predictable, so I chose *The Hunger Games*. It was soon to be a movie, so I thought it was offbeat yet should be familiar to them. The themes from the book lend themselves to talking about leadership - preparing yourself for the future, developing skills, taking risks, making decisions, and surviving in spite of incredible obstacles. So even having limited prep time, I felt good about the choice.

When I announced the name of the book, I received an immediate frown from one of the interviewers that lingered like a storm cloud for my entire presentation. My guess was that she had expected me to choose a professional book and not fiction, especially popular fiction aimed at young adults. Although I pushed on, it was clear that being creative wasn't what they were looking for. Although they acknowledged that I had some good ideas, it would have been better if I had put sugar instead of an exotic topping on my bowl of leadership porridge."

WINNING MOVES:

If what they *expect* is vanilla ice cream and you give them mango sorbet, they might be pleasantly surprised. But if what they *want* is vanilla ice cream and you give them mango sorbet, you are SOL (using the polite forms of IMglish, you are short on luck, sadly outta luck, or sorta outta luck). Sad but true.

AUNI?

"The team was anxiously awaiting a candidate for a group interview. It was a critical, tech position and one that had been hard to fill. Our department cubicles looked out over the parking lot, so when an unfamiliar and very fancy BMW sports car, a Z3, pulled up out front, it got everyone's attention. In no time at all the entire team was standing in front of the window staring at the car and its license plate: AUNI.

The conversation went something like this:

'AU – isn't that the symbol for gold?'

'I think it also stands for the African Union.'

'Well, NI is a chemical element, Nickel.'

'So…gold–nickel, what does that mean?'

'He could be in a band.'

'Maybe it's just initials…alluring undies…'

'Awesome undies…'

He stayed in his car for a while, giving us plenty of time to speculate. Although we never got past words beginning with 'a' and 'u.' When he finally got out we tried to assess the meaning of the license plate based on our first impression of him. He looked so 'normal.' Medium brown hair, medium height, bland clothes, carrying a briefcase. Definitely coming to our building for an interview. And difficult to picture in anything but boxers.

Once the interview was under way and things seemed to be going well, we could hardly contain ourselves. Finally someone asked the only question that had been on everyone's mind: 'What does AUNI mean?'

He was definitely pleased we had asked. 'GoldenEye,' he said with a smile. Mystery solved. And we hired him. The place needed a little class."

> **WINNING MOVES:**
> IGYHTBT (I guess you had to be there).

Conclusion:

For some the group interview is little more than a speed bump on the road to getting a job. But for others, it can feel like a huge pothole, something that not only shakes you up but that brings you to a complete stop. Definitely a WM (why me?!) OMG situation. And there doesn't seem to be any indication that the group interview will be going away any time soon, although it will undoubtedly continue to evolve. Probably the best advice for coping with the group interview is that given by Denis Waitley – not intended specifically for interviews, but definitely relevant: *"Expect the best, plan for the worst, and prepare to be surprised."* WFM (works for me).

LESSONS LEARNED THE EASY WAY
(Through Someone Else's Experience)

Group Interviews: Group interviews are intended to gauge culture fit, interpersonal skills, and, sometimes, individual and team problem solving. They can present challenges for both participants and observers.

- *Don't try to upstage other participants.*
  You may be tempted to want to show off your expertise in an area, but your communication with other participants may be as much or more important to your evaluators as your knowledge. Try to be an active participant while demonstrating that you have good listening skills.

- *Identify the people in the room.*
  If you are one of the interviewers, make sure the candidates know who is in the room and what their role is. If you are an interviewee, ask for introductions if they are not offered. You can't adapt to your audience if you don't know who the players are.

- *If you are an interviewer, let participants know the purpose of an activity.*
  If you want a "fun" person who can go with the flow, then it may make sense to throw a strange activity at a group and see how people react. Otherwise, a brief explanation of purpose can encourage people to do their best.

- *If you are a candidate, don't hesitate to ask the purpose of an activity.*
  If you want to know the purpose of a particular activity, ask. They will either explain or tell you that "guessing" is part of the purpose or that they will explain afterwards. At least you will know where you stand.

- *Accept that you can't please everyone.*
  You may come up with a great idea and deliver it perfectly; yet one or more of the interviewers may not be enthralled with your choice. Unfortunately, that's something you won't know until you try.

15
Once Upon an Interview

Once upon a time someone went on the interview circuit hoping to get a job or to be granted whatever it was they were seeking. They of course encountered some obstacles along the way, including the occasional monster. But holding fast to their purpose, they persevered, achieved their goal, and lived happily ever after. End of story. Or not–.

I've commented on the fairy tale characteristics after each story in this chapter. But, as you will discover, the last three stories are not the same as the other stories in this chapter or in the rest of the book. In two of them, obtaining a pet and not a job is the goal. And in the final story, well, you'll have to read it to see for yourself.

Hidden agenda

"Several years before I applied for a job at a large, local company, my position had been eliminated at a previous job. I never made it past the recruiter interview, but not for any of the reasons I speculated about at the time.

During my interview, the recruiter kept asking me about the position that had been eliminated. I was honest with her. I explained that, at the time, they didn't think I was strategic enough and also that they felt the position didn't add value to the organization. I went on to explain that I had learned a lot since then through the different positions I had held. I was therefore startled when she came back at me with, '*Don't you think it was your role to be strategic and to prove your value to the organization?'* I responded calmly with what I thought to be a fair and accurate assessment, but she didn't let up. She came back at the same question from another direction and continued to ask the same question in so many different ways with such negativity that it felt like she was making a statement – *YOU failed* – rather than trying to understand the situation or how I had changed since then.

When the interview ended, I knew I wasn't going to move on to the next level, but I wasn't entirely sure why.

Later I made two discoveries. First, at the time of my interview, the position had already been filled; they were looking for a back-up just in case something went wrong. Second, the recruiter was a friend of someone I had been in competition with (and beaten) for a previous job. The person got another job in the same organization, and as our paths continued to cross, it was clear that she never forgave me for getting the job that should have been hers.

Did the recruiter give my application serious consideration? Or was she making a statement on behalf of her friend? I will never know."

WINNING MOVES:
Let's see – a quest (check), a possible monster (check), obstacles (check). Okay, so sometimes the "happily ever after" doesn't happen.

Translation, please

"As a hospital administrator in a small town in a remote area of Alaska, the staff was mostly Yupik and did not speak English. So when hiring staff I had to rely on my bi-lingual head housekeeper, Florence, to translate for me. Every time we had to interview someone I felt like I was in a movie or a classic television show. I would tell her the question I wanted to ask and she would ask the candidate the question. The length of her question never seemed to have any relationship to what I had asked. Nor, frequently, did the response. My question might be a single sentence, and she would talk for two or three minutes before pausing for an answer. This would happen even if the question was supposed to elicit either a yes or a no. And even though I didn't know the language, I was pretty sure it shouldn't take the candidate two minutes to say 'yes' or 'no.'

My guess is that what she did was chat the person up, decided whether she liked them, and then made her recommendation on the basis of that. Or maybe she had already decided and they were just talking about the weather. I'll never know. But the people 'we' hired were always good workers, so it probably didn't make any difference.

That was how I honed my interview skills."

WINNING MOVES:
Quest (check). Fairy godmother (check). Happy ending (check).

Rough around the edges

"OK, here is my story...

I worked as an HR Manager for a large specialty retailer, where turnover was especially high. As a result, I spent much of my time staffing stores. So it wasn't unusual for me to run across people from time to time that society would deem as 'rough around the edges.' For as many bizarre experiences as I had (a mother coming into the store and screaming at me for not hiring her 18-year old son, an applicant asking if I would consider him since he just got out of prison for murdering his neighbor, etc.), there was one that, to this day, still amazes me.

During the behavioral interview, this particular candidate was asked to describe a time where he had to manage a conflict with another employee – what happened, how he responded, and what was the outcome. As the assistant manager and I listened, the candidate shared an experience he had working in a mine, where his boss became so angry with him (no explanation given) that the boss punched the candidate in his face. As the candidate continued the story, he explained how proud he was that he decided not to punch his boss in return even though his nose was broken and blood was gushing from his face. Stunned, I took a minute to gather my thoughts, knowing the interview had officially ended in my mind. After thanking the candidate for his time and escorting him out of my office, I returned to my office to debrief with my assistant manager. Before I could even open my mouth, the assistant manager asked, 'When can we hire him?'

Ah, but the story gets better. There's an old saying about giving people enough rope to hang themselves, and I knew this was the case. After I gave all my reasons as to why we should NOT hire him, the assistant manager still wanted to proceed, so I decided to give him exactly what he wanted. The next day I made the offer, and the candidate was thrilled – understandably. When he came into my office later that day to fill out his background check consent form, he asked if I would be in contact with his ex-wife, located in another state. I wondered 'why' so I asked, 'Why?' The candidate said, 'Well, she doesn't know where I am and I want to keep it that way – there are people looking for me.'

At this point I started to think there was something seriously wrong here, and, if I got out of this alive, I was not going to try this tactic to teach a manager a lesson ever again – I got the message. But I was now committed to complete the task of hiring this candidate, so my only hope (and fear) was that he would fail his background and/or drug test. For a week I waited for the results, and every day for that week, the candidate physically came to visit me to find out if his background check had cleared. At every visit, he became more and more agitated, and I was becoming the target of his anger. Like a blessing and a curse, the results finally came back…he failed the background check due to several felonies, violent in nature (mind you, he was being hired for a sales job). In addition, there was a warrant for his arrest from another state, the same state where his ex-wife resided.

The rest of the story is really a blur. There was something in there about me notifying him, giving him the number of the vendor in case he wanted to contest the results, then changing my work hours, taking down my posted schedule, and parking in different locations around the parking lot. What I do remember clearly is the assistant manager's response when I shared the full results of the background check: *'Isn't there anything we can do?'"*

> **WINNING MOVES:**
> Yes – there IS something they could do: not hire him! This is definitely a story where the protagonist failed to learn from the experience. A failed fairy tale.

Serendipity

"Some people search for jobs for months, even years. It can be a very discouraging process. But one man I know got a very good job by finding a flyer advertising a position he didn't know was available. He found it on the mailroom floor and was just picking it up to be tidy. It was the last day to apply. He did, and the rest is history."

> **WINNING MOVES:**
> This story started with the happy ending, proving the statement that life isn't fair. Some people have to face the complications and obstacles before achieving their goal.

Wrong number

As told by the interviewer:

"I was starting a new software center to assist a multinational software company in supporting some new chip architecture. They gave me an on-site office, but didn't change the voice mail for the telephone. When I realized there was a message on it, I listened to see whether it was something I needed to pass along to someone. The message was from a job applicant. He talked about his interest and qualifications for a position at Microsoft. There was something about him that I liked, so I decided to respond directly."

As told by the interviewee:

"When I got the call about a potential interview from someone I had not contacted, I was surprised. She told me that she had heard my message, liked what I had said, and believed in fate. She explained that she was starting a software center and needed someone to manage it and to build the relationship with Microsoft. She had reached out to me because she felt it was an alignment of the stars that enabled her to get the voice message from me in the first place.

I told her that I, too, believed in fate, even though at the time I left the message I had been very interested in the other position. We set up a time to meet, and I ended up accepting a job that I stayed with for six years. During that time I had the opportunity to do some similar work for another large company, and that in turn lead me to my current position. It all happened because of a phone call intercepted by the wrong person. But I credit both my career course and professional success to that call."

WINNING MOVES:
This story could be categorized as a "happy accident," but the convergence of coincidences lends a magical quality, something outside of what usually happens under normal conditions. Or maybe it's just an excellent example of how six degrees of separation can manifest itself.

The curious case of the outdoor cat

"When we went to the animal shelter to look for a cat I had no idea that I would be deemed an 'unfit parent.' Why, I had raised three kids, and over the years we had owned a number of cats. But the people at the animal shelter didn't care about that. I flunked their test.

'*Where do you intend to keep the cat?*' the woman asked.

'*In the house.*' That seemed to be an okay response because she asked another question.

'*Will the cat have its own space?*'

'*Yes.*' I could tell by the nod of the head that I'd scored another right answer.

'*Will you let it go outside?*'

I quickly replied, '*Yes.*' Easy question, or so I thought.

'*Then I'm afraid we can't let you have one of our cats.*'

I was so surprised that I argued with the woman about whether it was okay for a cat to go outside. Maybe I got a little rude, but I don't think that was any reason for them to put my answers on their computer. I was effectively blackballed from getting a cat even from another animal shelter!

After a number of tries at different locations, I finally had some luck. Either they didn't check their computer or were willing to give me a second chance based on me giving them the correct answers this time around. I adopted an indoor cat with its own room, and if occasionally she went outside for a little stroll, no one from the animal shelter had to know.

My cat lived a long, happy, and uneventful life – even when she ventured outside."

WINNING MOVES:

It's mind boggling to think that you have to prepare for an interview to obtain a pet. But maybe that's a good thing. Quest, complications, mini monster in the form of bureaucracy, and happy ending.

If you want a puppy–

"By the time I called the breeder I knew exactly what I wanted and that it was one of their puppies. I knew of several dogs that had come from that breeder and was really looking forward to having one of my own. But in spite of my enthusiasm I was told: '*I'm really busy; you can call back in six weeks if you are still interested.*'

Like clockwork, I called back in six weeks. This time I was informed that I could come by and look at her dogs. When I showed up the mother was in heat and wasn't paying any attention to people, but I wasn't dissuaded. I told them that I wanted a good companion dog and that I didn't care about color or gender, but the dog needed to be calm and sturdy. I thought I was being very reasonable and clear.

What I hadn't realized is that you don't 'order' a puppy from this breeder. You 'interview' with the breeder just like for a job. And even though you may be purchasing a very expensive puppy, the issue is not whether you can afford the dog but whether you will be accepted by the breeder. Only then can you get your name on a list of potential buyers. I'm happy to report that I figured that out in time and had a successful interview. Now I'm the proud owner of the perfect companion dog. You should see him–."

> **WINNING MOVES:**
> Another person learns from the quest and goes on to find a happy ending.

Not really an interview

"This wasn't an interview, but it came to mind when I was asked to think about interviews, and I love this story. It goes back a ways, to the 60s, but it's as vivid in my mind as if it happened yesterday.

This doctor had just completed his internship as a general practitioner and ended up in Barrow, Alaska, the 11th northernmost city in the world. Barrow's predominant land type is tundra that sits on permafrost that is as much as 1,300 feet deep. It is cold and dry and very isolated.

One night there was a screaming storm and a kid came in with appendicitis. Since our doc was not a surgeon, he called Anchorage to find out what to do. They told him to give the kid antibiotics and hopefully they would be able to fly him out the next day after the storm had settled out.

Unfortunately, the antibiotics didn't seem to do any good. And the storm continued. So the doctor who had never operated before decided the only alternative was to remove the kid's appendix.

He called Anchorage again and told them he was going to have to operate. There was no radio phone in the room where he needed to operate, so he set up a system that involved a surgery textbook and four nurses. The first nurse was there to assist him. The other three were positioned to relay messages from the radio to the temporary OR. One stood at the door to the OR. The next was down the hall at the corner of the corridor. And the remaining nurse was on the VHF radio to the surgeon in Anchorage. It went something like this...

'I'm ready to start,' said the doctor.
'He's ready to start,' said the nurse at the doorway.
'He's ready to start,' repeated the nurse in the hall.
'He's ready to start,' the last nurse tells the surgeon in Anchorage.

Directions are relayed back. Shortly into the procedure...

'I can't find the appendix.'
'He can't find the appendix.'
'He can't find the appendix.'
'He can't find the appendix.'
'Look behind the liver.'
'Look behind the liver.'
'Look behind the liver.'
'Still can't find the appendix.'
'He still can't find the appendix.'
'He still can't find the appendix.'
'He still can't find the appendix.'

This goes on for about thirty minutes. Finally he locates the appendix, removes it, and closes up. The kid survives. Later on they moved the radio closer to the surgery...just in case."

> **WINNING MOVES:**
> The person who told me this story has hired quite a few people during his career as a manager and executive. One of the things he says that he looks for in an employee is someone who is committed to doing whatever it takes to solve problems and overcome obstacles. And that, after all, is what fairy tales and interviews are all about.

Conclusion:

Fairy tales allow us to dream big and learn lessons through fantastical scenarios. Whereas interviews teach us lessons the hard way – through personal experience. And just like there are formulas for writing a fairy tale, there are also formulas or guidelines for preparing for and going through an interview or series of interviews. In both instances we dream big. We face and overcome obstacles. And, hopefully, there is a happy ending - for a time at least; even if we don't believe in "happily ever after" outside of fairy tales.

LESSONS LEARNED THE EASY WAY
(Through Someone Else's Experience)

Obstacles: You can anticipate some but not all of the obstacles you may encounter when trying to find a job or achieve a goal. The key is to figure out a way to overcome them in the moment.

- *Stay calm.*
  Even if you don't feel calm on the inside, it's always a good idea to appear to be calm. Especially if you sense that something is amiss. Losing your cool is not a winning move; it causes a chemical change in your brain that makes action easier but thinking more difficult.

- *Persist.*
  Sometimes our first reaction to an obstacle is to throw our hands in the air and give up. Instead, take a step back and see if there is a way over, around or through the obstacle. In other words, get creative and look for another route to your goal.

16
Crème de la Weird

There are a number of magazines, newspapers and online sources that publish news stories on bizarre or weird crime. They also publish lists of stupid things people say. (Like, *"It's always the last place you look."*) And stupid things people do. (Just check out what people have done by mistake with Super Glue!) Then, of course, there are the Darwin Awards given to people who unnecessarily put themselves in life-threatening situations and self-select themselves out of the gene pool.

The following are mostly stories about people who self-selected themselves out of the interview pool. Although some succeeded in landing the job in spite of what they said or did. Now *that's* beyond weird.

Undercover employee

"I was doing interviews for a collector position at a credit union in the late 90s. The applicant came in wearing a jeans jacket and holey jeans with her hair a mess and smelling like smoke. She had a raspy voice and a definite 'attitude.' I asked her what made her qualified for the job.

'Look,' she said. *'If I ever have to, I can go undercover.'*

'Undercover?' I asked. *'This isn't a law enforcement job.'*

'I know,' she replied, *'but my next door neighbor works at the police station, and she's a bitch. She needs to have her car repo'd! So if you need me to do it, I can be a diversion when the tow truck comes.'*

I didn't have a response for that, other than thanking her for her time."

> **WINNING MOVES:**
> Since *Candid Camera* went off the air it's hard to know what other possible explanations there are for behavior like this.

Clip, clip

"The candidate was a senior level technical leader who lacked interpersonal awareness. While waiting in the interview room, the candidate thought it would be a great idea to clip his fingernails ... onto the floor!!"

> **WINNING MOVES:**
> There's a thin line at times between weird and crude.

Hate to eat and run

"Back when I worked in the UK public sector, I ran a series of interview panels where we would interview hundreds of people a month prior to deciding who to put through into an assessment center. Although this was quite a few years ago, one candidate always comes easily to mind. He entered the room holding a half-eaten apple, which he then put on the desk in front of him. The first question we asked was to describe his last job (which was stated quite clearly on his resume in front of him and us).

He looked at his resume, looked at the interview panel, took a bite of his apple and chewed. After a minute, he looked at the interview panel and said, *'To be honest, I don't remember what that job was about, so I'll take this opportunity to just leave.'*

He then shook our hands, took his apple, and went!"

> **WINNING MOVES:**
> It makes you wonder if this was really the person with the resume or just someone who wandered in looking for a place to finish his lunch.

Dragon lady

"I was interviewing with a store HR manager. Things seemed to be going well. Then in the middle of the interview she pulled out her bright red fingernail polish and proceeded to paint her nails. Apparently I was quite boring and she was boorish...

Although I didn't get the job, I got another one in the same large retail company. So from time to time I would run into her. Whenever I saw her, I pictured her as the Dragon Lady with her extra long, bright red nails."

> **WINNING MOVES:**
> I wonder what would have happened if the interviewee had said, "Oh, love that color. Can I use it next?" Although maybe there isn't room in the same organization for two Dragon Ladies.

Wrong plan

"It was the last interview of the day for an engineering position. The guy had flown in that morning, and something he said made me wonder if he had been waiting in the airport all day. As we got into the interview I was convinced he HAD been in the airport all day - at the *bar*. In response to an engineering plan review question, he explained in detail the drainage shown for this two-lane road on the chart in front of him. That would have been fine, but it was actually a drawing of a six-lane major arterial!"

> **WINNING MOVES:**
> But he had practiced for his interview explaining drainage for a two-lane road! Or maybe he misplaced his glasses at the bar.

Analyze THAT

"There's an INFAMOUS company in a major metropolitan area that follows some of the most goofy interview techniques I've ever heard in my life. I've had many clients interview there. Their experiences range from the interviewer pretending to be drunk on tequila and making racial slurs to having two workers come in and start a fistfight. I suppose the goal is to see how the candidate handles pressure or something along those lines, but these scenarios are SO bizarre I honestly have no idea what their motivation might be. Literally, their interview approach is the most unusual I've ever come across."

> **WINNING MOVES:**
> Under these circumstances do you call HR, 911 or the etiquette police?

Do you not want this job?!

"Over the years I've had some strange questions from people that I've interviewed. One typical but still unacceptable question is: *How many questions do you have?!* This is always expressed with a tone that implies they can't believe how many questions I'm asking. Another of my favorites is: *What kind of position is this, anyway?!* Oh, just the one you applied for–.

Perhaps my all-time favorite experience with strange questions came from a young woman who was avoiding eye contact with everyone in the room. And she was obviously having trouble answering our questions. So in response to one, she looked at the painting on the wall and asked, '*What kind of painting is that?*' Then in response to our next question she said, '*I wonder what the weather will be like later?*'

If you are interviewing to fulfill a quota, these are show stoppers. You get your checkmark but not the job. But you better not apply again when the unemployment payments run out–."

> **WINNING MOVES:**
> It's a bit like trying not to get selected for a jury. I had been called up and found myself sitting next to another potential juror who was wearing a sleeveless T-shirt and flip-flops. He said he'd read that no attorney wanted a juror dressed like that. If that didn't work he was going to say something to demonstrate his bias. For some it's a toss-up between looking stupid or saying something stupid.

Just what the government needs

"We had an internal candidate for a position who came into the interview with a huge pile of papers. We asked all of the routine questions. Then we couldn't stand it and asked why all of the paperwork. '*When my boss comes around,*' she explained, '*I want to look busy. So I always have a stack of papers handy to rifle through.*' One of the other interviewers then asked if she had enough to do on her job. '*Sure,*' she replied. '*And if I don't have enough, I make some up.*'

She was dead serious. We decided not to give her the opportunity to bring her stack of papers to our corner of the world. We actually believe in government service."

> **WINNING MOVES:**
> She managed to both do, and say, something stupid simultaneously. A home run.

To text or not to text

"We were hiring for a mortgage originator, and the mortgage manager and I were conducting the interviews. In one interview, we had a candidate who was texting throughout the entire interview. He acted like we could not see what he was doing. Although it did not stop him from answering our questions, it was extremely bizarre.

Then to top it off, the manager decided she wanted to hire the 'texting' candidate. She explained that she would tell him to never text while meeting with a member. Astonished, I asked, *'Why do you want to hire someone when your first conversation is telling them not to text with a member?'* In my experience, if someone is going to text during an interview, they are going to text in other inappropriate situations. It took some convincing, but we did not hire this candidate."

WINNING MOVES:

Texting while doing other things has become an epidemic among some groups. I know a facilitator who had someone text her during a workshop. Since she had her cell turned off, she didn't get the text until later. By then it was no longer relevant, since the individual had been asking for clarification about something she had just said. Apparently it was easier to text than to raise his hand.

Lookin' good

"I was being interviewed for a high-end matchmaking job. Just as the owner was telling me how classy, rich, and high-end the clients were, one of her clients barged in and ripped off his shirt to show her that, even though he was older (65-ish), he was in tip-top shape and wasn't terribly pleased about her matching him up with 'fat old fanny-pack-wearing hippie ladies.'

He then turned to me and asked, *'Are you single?'*

He was the director of some lauded indie films and quite full of himself. High-end, perhaps. However, I wasn't impressed. I've seen better chests with less hair.

I did get the job, btw."

WINNING MOVES:
What can I say – fanny-packs *are* passé.

Darwin Award for interviewing

"I was making small talk at a party, when someone brought up an interview that took place at a large, international company. As someone who has done a lot of interviewing over the years, I was stunned by what this person said happened.

The husband already worked there, so when he heard about a position that had opened up, he submitted a resume for his wife and managed to get her an interview.

About half way through the interview the wife asked the interviewers, *'Why do you keep calling me Clara?'*

Apparently the resume submitted by her husband was not his wife's resume, but someone named Clara. He hadn't even bothered to change the name. Or to warn his wife.

Now neither works for the company."

WINNING MOVES:
My question is whether they are still married…

Conclusion:

It's difficult to know where to draw the line between funny and just plain weird. The first chapter focused on stories I labeled as "humorous," but some might consider them weird. There is a saying, *Everybody is someone else's weirdo.* In some ways it's a question of point of view. We tend to empathize with the person telling the story – whether their actions are outside of our comfort level or not. At the same time, we celebrate the offbeat and wacky in movies and television programs, on YouTube and Facebook, even in the photos we share on our cell phones. Whether it's humor or weirdness, if it gives us an excuse to smile or laugh, to share in the messiness that is life, then from my perspective, it doesn't matter what we label it.

LESSONS LEARNED THE EASY WAY
(Through Someone Else's Experience)

Weird Interviews: Don't self-select yourself out of the interview pool by doing something that people will want to tweet or blog about.

- *Don't take food into an interview. Water or tea is okay.*
  No one looks their best when eating. So if you need something to eat, do it before going in for the interview. And before you are seated in a lobby where people can be checking you out. Coffee has a chemical in it that dries the throat; so it's best to avoid coffee immediately before or during an interview.

- *Don't waste the interviewers' time.*
  If you really don't want the job, don't accept the offer of an interview. The job market isn't as big as you might think, and people move around. You may eventually apply for a job you want and find yourself face-to-face with someone you previously blew off.

- *Turn off your telephone during an interview!*
  You need to give your interviewer(s) your full attention. It may be acceptable in some circles to say, "Oh, I have to take this–," but not in an interview.

- *Use common sense.*
  There is sometimes a thin line between being amusing or just whacky. Keep in mind how important first impressions can be, and try not to cross the line.

17

Slacklining: The Art & Science of Interviewing

You may be familiar with slacklining, a balance sport in which someone walks a flat strip of line stretched between two anchor points. The fact that the line is flat keeps the slacker's foot from simply rolling off. Still, staying on the line is not easy, and getting bucked off as the line moves up and down with each wobbly step is not uncommon.

Interviews are a kind of *mental* slacklining, on both sides of the interview table. Although from the interviewee's perspective it may seem like the role of the interviewer is to simply watch and wait for a misstep, everyone in the process walks a bouncy line. Interviewees try to stay calm and focus on getting from point A to point B, hoping there won't be any surprises to throw them off balance and require a forced dismount. For HR, on the other hand, it's a balancing act between the need to quickly fill positions and finding the "right" person while maintaining respectful relationships with both internal clients and job applicants.

In this chapter there are no stories. Rather, it's an exploration of this balancing act, primarily from the HR perspective, in order help both sides cope with the sometimes unwieldy and always stressful interview process.

One reason HR walks a bouncy line is that many people hold a traditional view of its function as one that focuses primarily on "soft issues" associated with managing, nurturing and developing employees. This vision of HR creates specific expectations about the interactions between recruiters and internal clients as well as between recruiters and job seekers. Recruiters are expected to be not only friendly and efficient, but supportive, accommodating and available. And, although most recruiters would agree that these qualities are important, they know that they will ultimately be evaluated on the cost and business drivers associated with the interview process.

In this chapter I first take a look at two sets of metrics that can, and usually *do,* have a profound influence on the hiring process: cost-per-hire and time-to-fill. Having some knowledge of these behind-the-scenes measurements can help the interviewee understand the larger business context within which their very personal experience is taking place. Next, I take a brief look at future workplace trends that are possibly going to change not only the workplace itself, but how people are recruited, evaluated, and hired. This will be important for both interviewees and interviewers going forward. Finally, so many of the stories in this book focus on the questions asked in the interviews that I feel a need to touch on some of the more interesting aspects of the art and science of the interview question. Although this is not intended to be a thorough review of how to create or respond to interview questions, I'm hoping that the discussion will provide some useful insight to those asking the questions as well as to those trying to answer them.

The HR Moonwalk

For the fleet of foot, there are some innovative ways to maneuver on the slackline. One is the moonwalk, the illusion that someone is gliding backwards while seemingly trying to move forward. That can be how it feels to an HR person searching for qualified candidates while being held accountable for all of the costs associated with the process.

It's obviously in everyone's best interest to fill a position as quickly as possible. The company wants to maintain an adequate level of staffing to ensure on-going productivity. A team with a vacant position needs another body to do the work. The recruiter wants to demonstrate that they can find qualified candidates in a timely manner. And the interviewee wants to get hired. This should be a straightforward, linear process, but that isn't necessarily how it plays out.

One of the factors that complicates the process is the cost-to-hire metric. Simply stated, the cost-to-hire ratio is the average of all expenses incurred during the hiring process divided by the number of new hires. This includes external expenses such as advertising, third-party agency fees, job fair costs, travel associated with recruiting, outsourced background checks, and internal expenses such as staffing time and infrastructure. Any way you slice it, it adds up to a lot of money. For example, the SHRM (Society for Human Resource Management) Benchmarking Database for 2011-2012 estimates that at the high end the average cost-per-hire for professional/trade is $5,582 and at the low end for arts and recreation, the average is $1,394. Of course it costs more to hire an executive than nonexempt staff. And large organizations spend more than smaller organizations to bring someone on board. SHRM recently created a standard formula and methodology for determining costs associated with the hiring process. But however you measure it, emphasizing cost over quality can result in perfunctory interviews, inadequate follow-up with candidates and poor hiring decisions.

In addition to the cost-per-hire metric, management usually tracks turnover costs. These include the direct costs of replacement, including paperwork, as well as the indirect costs of decreases in production, overtime pay, morale issues during transition that may impact performance, time to fill issues, etc. So if turnover is high, that's ironically treated as still another reason to keep cost-per-hire low. It is usually estimated that the cost of turnover to a for-profit company is up to 150% of the employees' salary package. The 2011 *BenchmarkPro* survey found companies were experiencing turnover rates of 14.4 percent between 2010 and 2011. These rates vary by industry with higher turnover in organizations with a lot of entry-level positions and the lowest for utilities employers (6.2 percent). Although HR is not directly responsible for turnover rates, the cost of turnover impacts the demands placed on HR by those wanting to fill positions quickly.

That brings us to timing, another critical element that puts pressure on the process. The standard goal is to hire in "less than thirty days," but SHRM research estimates the average time to fill per position in 2011 was 33.28 days. (Time to fill is calculated from the time a job requisition is submitted until the offer is accepted by a candidate.) Variables include forecasting, recruiter availability, the market, expertise needed, and talent supply. Large organizations had a higher average time-to-fill, 43 days, compared with 29 days for smaller organizations. The assumption for this difference is that large organizations have more structured processes, hire more people, may have additional testing, and involve more people in the approval process. Whether looking at cost-per-hire, turnover, or time-to-fill, there is a lot of money at stake. And the stress of trying to keep costs low can cause that slackline to bounce and buck.

Discussing the pressure metrics put on the hiring process is not intended to excuse recruiters and hiring managers who treat candidates poorly. But many of the online complaints made by applicants are about a lack of communication during the process. This isn't necessarily an intentional act of discourtesy; it could be a time issue. By understanding the context within which the interviews are scheduled, conducted and concluded, perhaps both "sides" can find ways to maintain their balance while traversing the slackline.

The Buddha Sit

The Buddha Sit of slacklining mimics the position Buddha is depicted in when meditating and clearing his mind. Although I'm not certain how conducive that position is to meditation when on a slackline, the original objective of this Zen posture is to create a peaceful state of mind where one can see connections between ideas and the physical world. Whether they meditate or not, HR folks may be in need of some clear-headed thinking in order to reconcile hiring practices with a changing workforce. Similarly, interviewees competing in this new environment will need to make adjustments. Just think (with a clear mind) how both jobs and the process of hiring people to fill these jobs will have to adapt to meet the challenges of the following facts:

1. According to the Pew Research Center, 10,000 baby boomers will turn 65 every day for the next 18 years.
2. By 2015 half of the boomer population will be 60.
3. In general, roughly 25% of managers in an organization transition into a new role each year; each transition has a ripple effect.
4. When any leader – formal or informal – leaves a team, productivity is disrupted.
5. Many organizations either don't have succession plans at all or don't have them below the executive level (it is estimated that only about 35% have succession plans).
6. Most organizations have either an onboarding and/or orientation program but lack a structured approach to managing gaps while leaders and team members are being replaced.
7. Younger employees may see jobs as transitory, increasing the turnover rate. According to a survey by Future Workplace (Multiple Generations@Work), 91 percent of millennials (born between 1977-1997) expect to stay in a job for less than three years.

There is no way to know which of these trends will have the greatest impact on the interviewing and hiring process. But one thing is certain, connecting the dots will take a great deal of time and effort, causing a lot of stress on BOTH sides of the interview process.

Freestyle

Freestyle slacklining is walking on a line that is draped slack rather than tensioned. Thus it is able to swing more, creating a different dynamic from standard slacklining. Often times interviewers treat the questioning process as a freestyle event with managers and recruiters convinced that if they can just ask the right set of questions they will be able to predict whether the candidate will succeed in the role they applied for. Unfortunately, the interviewing skills of the candidate are not necessarily aligned with the skills needed on the job. Some people interview really well but can't perform, and vice versa. At the same time, research and common sense tells us, there is no way to consistently predict success with certainty, no matter how creative interviewers get with their questions.

Nevertheless, when I see article titles like "Three Questions that Reveal Everything" or "Top Executive Recruiters Agree There Are Only Three True Job Interview Questions," I can't resist at least browsing the article. Usually the questions recommended in these articles have two main goals: to determine fit and to get past the interview gloss to potential performance. Although most of these articles fall far short of the promise in their titles, occasionally there's a useful tidbit.

After taking a look at the more traditional ways to address questions and answers in interviews, I'll share one of the tidbits I came across recently and then discuss the issues surrounding the interviewee's opportunity to ask questions at the end of the interview. All of these topics have interesting and potentially serious implications for the art and science of interviewing.

If art represents the creative and exploratory side of interviewing and science the fact and order side, then obviously we need both if we are to have an effective interview process. Almost everyone is aware of the two types of interview questions used by most interviewers: situational and behavioral. With situational questions, candidates are asked to respond to hypothetical situations and explain what they would do given a particular set of *facts*. The situations may be brief or elaborate. An example of an elaborate situational question is the in-box activity described in Chapter Eleven (*Doing Not Telling*). Behavioral questions, on the other hand, assume that past behavior is the best predictor of future behavior, so they focus on what the candidate has done in the past. This gives the individual license to cherry pick from their experiences to *create* the best way of arguing for their candidacy.

Since research has been unable to determine which type of questions are the best predictors of performance, the safest bet for HR is to use a variety of questions and spend time engaging the candidate in conversations that provide a general feel for the candidate's abilities, work style, and approach to problem solving. And just in case, interviewees have to be prepared for both types of questions.

There is also a category sometimes labeled "stress questions or situations." Not surprisingly, a lot of stress stories found their way into this book. They included candidates being asked to solve a puzzle, make a presentation with limited time to prepare, and being asked to participate in a group "competition." In these situations, candidates had to rely on art, science and just plain luck to get through.

Although some interviewees seemed to enjoy the challenge of the stress question or situation, most tended to relate their experience through a negative lens. I've used stress questions/situations myself and have mixed feelings about whether it's a good idea or not. If the position requires someone who can think on their feet and roll with the punches, then this may be a legitimate form of evaluation. But some people need time to process ideas and situations, and ruling them out as employees because they aren't "fun" or "quick" could be a mistake.

Many people consider the panel interview to be a "stress" situation. They can definitely be intimidating to candidates. However, from a hiring manager's perspective, the panel interview is one of the best ways to get team buy-in for a new employee. What has surprised me over the years, however, is how different some people can be in the one-on-one versus a group interview. So having a mix of interview settings before making a final decision can provide information about the individual's knowledge as well as how they behave in groups. That said, HR has some special obligations when overseeing panel interviews. It's critical that panels are carefully orchestrated to put candidates at ease (as much as possible), to ensure consistency in how candidates are treated, and to avoid crossing any legal boundaries.

As I mentioned earlier, someone is always coming up with something that they label as a new approach, even though most have been tried before under a different name. Yet, one online article I read recently has stayed with me for its simplicity and cunning. The author suggested that one should go down the work history of the individual and ask the same three questions about each position they've held: 1) How did you find out about the job? 2) What did you like about the job before you started? and 3) Why did you leave? The assumption is that the answers from these three questions will enable the person asking the questions to determine how self-reflective the candidate is and how much they want the particular job. If they just apply for jobs the same old way each time and don't learn through their network about openings, then supposedly they aren't the best candidates. Also, if they don't know what kind of environment they do best in, then how do you know if they will be a good fit for your organization? Of course as an interviewer, you are also looking for patterns with these questions. And you may indeed find them. Although I'm not sure every open position lends itself to this approach, I think repeating the same set of questions may indeed yield interesting comparative results. Conversely, if you are about to go for an interview, you might want to think about how you would answer this series of questions!

Although I hesitate to mimic some of those catchy headlines I referred to at the beginning of this section, the bottom line is that three questions are the foundation for all of the questions asked in most interviews: 1) Can you DO the job? 2) Will you LIKE doing the job? and 3) Will WE like working with you? That comes down to skills, engagement, and relationships. If you are interviewing for a position, it might be helpful to think about potential questions from these three perspectives. And, if you are conducting the interview, you might find it helpful to categorize questions under these three headings so you can assess strengths and potential gaps. Then, given the requirements of the particular job, you can decide how important the strengths and gaps are.

There's one more angle on the question and answer part of interviewing that sometimes determines whether someone is hired or not, and that is what questions the candidates asks at the end of the interview. If a candidate says that they don't have any questions, most interviewers consider that tantamount to saying that they don't really want the job. On the other hand, when questions are asked about information that is available on the company website, most interviewers feel like responding is a waste of time.

Nor do most interviewers like to spend time answering detailed questions about what the person could expect on the job when no decision to hire has been made. The best advice for the interviewee is to come with a list of questions but be alert to both time and nonverbal cues when deciding what to ask.

Since the interviewers are responsible for the nature and type of questions asked during the main part of the interview, the interviewee must prepare for as many contingencies as possible. My advice to interviewees? Whether the slackline is over water, 20 or 2 feet off the ground, taut or draped, take a deep breath, stretch your arms out wide, and go for it!

180 Jump Turns

As we strive to improve the often flawed and cumbersome interview process, we need to think about those current trends and what kinds of questions might arise on both sides of the table. Unlike the slackliner who does a 180 jump turn simply to prove they can do it, both HR and job candidates must be prepared to change directions just because what works today may not work tomorrow. Recruiters and hiring managers need to seek new approaches and creative ways to gather the information needed from candidates in order to make good choices. And candidates need to be thoughtful about what they want from a position and strategize about their on-the-job requirements. For example:

From the interviewee's perspective
1. What are my opportunities for development and growth?
2. Will I be able to do flex scheduling or telecommute?
3. Does the company encourage work/life balance?
4. Do I think I'm a good "fit" for their culture and for this position?

From the company's perspective
1. Do we need to make our interviewing more informal and social media focused to attract Millenials?

2. Do we need to consider potential job share positions to retain and/ or attract baby boomers?
3. Are we prepared to let go of our 24/7 mentality in order to fill management positions with younger employees?
4. Does our employee brand clearly reflect our culture?

These questions grapple with issues that impact both the art and the science of interviewing from the two perspectives. As organizations adapt to the expectations of a changing workforce, they do so with one eye on the bottom line. We know (or think we do) what the next generation of workers expect from jobs and careers. But at the same time, HR must be nimble enough to change direction when the facts dictate that we should – perhaps not 180 jump turns, but whatever moves it takes to provide a desirable work environment while maintaining and even growing productivity.

Candidates, on the other hand, must learn to be realistic yet forward-looking in their expectations of what's possible in the workplace. By asking about the issues they care about, they not only determine whether they want the particular job, they signal HR as to what is important to them.

Conclusion:
In spite of all the variables and changes taking place, one thing will undoubtedly remain the same: the stress caused by interviewing. We will need to keep telling our stories to make sure we put these experiences in perspective. As Kurt Vonnegut said, "We have to continually be jumping off cliffs and developing our wings on the way down." That's the only way we will all survive the slackline bounce.

18

The Inhale

"Comedy is defiance. It's a snort of contempt in the face of fear and anxiety. And it's the laughter that allows hope to creep back on the inhale." Will Durst

When we are looking for a different job or trying to find a job, any job, there is more at stake than just a paycheck. Most of us tend to identify with our work. We go to a party and ask others, "What do you do?" We assume that by getting the answer to that one question, we will know enough about the other person to carry on a conversation. For, at some level, our work becomes an integral part of our self-identity, the way we see ourselves as well as how others see us. Supposedly this is less true of Millenials who are said to think of themselves as mobile skill sets. Yet many Millenials go into traditional jobs, and for those who don't, there may still come a point at which the ability to excel at a task that must be performed on a regular basis becomes at least part of a definition of self and self-worth.

There's a training exercise that uses the sentence starter "I am..." as a lead-in to talking about how we see ourselves. You ask participants to take a few minutes to complete the sentence starting with "I am..." in as many ways as they can think of. Responses from people of all ages and different professions usually include basic information such as: "I am...." a woman/man, a mother/father, a sister/brother. Or descriptors such as "I am..." smart, impatient, loving, energetic, a good team member, an unappreciated employee, etc. But what someone does for employment is almost always one of the first things listed. Anecdotally at least, this exercise suggests that we *are* what we spend a good deal of our time *doing*.

In the classic book, *Point of No Return* by John Marquand, the main character, while waiting to hear whether he got a promotion, reflects on what might have been if he had made different choices. He speculates on how his career shaped not only his professional but his personal life. As he, and we, close one door, another may open, but at some point there are fewer doors left to open – and those that are left are harder to open without a great deal of effort.

In the best times, our jobs give us both a sense of meaning and fulfillment. But they can also be a source of insecurity, stress, and low self-esteem. We can be grateful just to have a job, or feel trapped by having a particular job. We can aspire to "move up" in an organization or simply want to be left alone to do what we were hired to do. Whatever the situation, there is definitely more involved than just a paycheck.

Demystifying interview stress

It has been said that stress is when you wake up screaming and then realize you haven't fallen asleep yet. Although some people claim they do their best work when under stress, that's not how it pencils out statistically. You've probably seen the humongous estimates on what stress costs American businesses each year in health care costs. Undoubtedly you have personally experienced the exhaustion that follows periods of high stress. That's your body's way of telling you to either take a break or, in some instances, to "inhale."

Demystifying what stress is and accepting the fact that it will occur before and during the interview is the first step to dealing with it. Notice that I did not use the word "control" or even "manage." Any time you present to an audience, whether one-on-one or to a group, your body chemistry kicks in and tries to give you the energy to cope. It's the old "fight or flight" survival trait coming to your rescue. We usually label it as nervousness. And nervousness produces stress.

One important thing to remember is that your nervousness isn't as obvious to everyone else as it is to you. You may feel your heart pounding, but no one else can hear it. You may think that everyone is aware of your shaky knees or sweaty palms, but chances are they are focused elsewhere.

And they definitely can't "see" your uncomfortable feelings or mental panic. Unless you call attention to these things yourself, which job candidates often do. Sometimes they make an unplanned, spur of the moment comment about being nervous; other times they may refer to their nervousness to enlist sympathy for their situation. But although interviewers may understand and even feel sorry that someone is nervous, most prefer self-confidence to honesty.

One time when teaching a presentation skills class I decided that it would be helpful if everyone thought about what could go wrong so they would realize there was nothing that they couldn't handle. I began by sharing stories with them, stories like the following:

1. It was a first-time presentation to a large audience of several hundred people. My friend bought a new suit and new shoes because she wanted to look her best. When her feet started to hurt she felt it was safe to slip off her shoes because she was speaking from behind a podium. Of course she didn't anticipate that her feet would swell and she wouldn't be able to simply slip her shoes back on. Nor did she notice the price tag hanging from a spot under her sleeve, a tag that swung back and forth as she gestured. But everyone else did.

2. I thought it was cool to speak from a stool. Unfortunately, I hooked my high heels behind one of the rungs. So when I used a large gesture that threw me off balance, I went down as the stool toppled over.

3. While making a presentation on a raised stage and writing on a whiteboard that ran the length of the platform and a bit beyond it, the speaker stepped off the edge and fell. (Fortunately, she did not hurt herself...physically.)

4. The speech was boring. Each time the presenter turned to write something on the whiteboard, a few more people left the room. (And this was a well-known author, an expert in his field.)

5. He was prepared to give his speech from notes, but he took the wrong notes up with him.

6. He needed his speaking notes, failed to number them, and they slid off the podium and scattered across the floor.

They groaned at the examples, but when I asked what the presenters should have done under the circumstances, they came up with lots of ideas to salvage each situation.

I didn't know it at the time, but I was trying to help them practice Ehrenreich's theory of "defensive pessimism" to prepare them for "dire possibilities." Although the exercise may have worked for some, I was assured by a number of participants that it only heightened their nervousness. One woman told me that for days before her presentation that she was focused like a laser on those ten minutes when she would be in front of the group. And there was nothing I could say or do to make it any better. Nonetheless, for me, considering the worst thing that can happen is an essential part of disaster preparedness.

Inhaling and other coping mechanisms

There are a ton of self-help books out there on how to cope with stress. They cover tactics to fit almost every need. You can read about how to avoid stress, how to manage or re-channel your stress once it happens, and how to make life-changing attitude adjustments in only seven steps. There's something for every occasion, just like a Hallmark card. The following isn't intended to be a definitive catalog of stress busters, but it includes some of the more popular, pragmatic techniques along with my comments on the challenges associated with using them. There may be no panacea for coping with stress, but creating your own patchwork quilt of remedies from what the experts have to offer is better than the alternative.

- Think big picture.
  Goal: Ask yourself if not getting this job will matter in a year, five years, ten years. Chances are you can remember other disappointments and disasters from the past that you no longer think are significant. That's supposed to be the reassuring part.

Challenges: The problem with this approach is that it assumes your answer to the question of whether it will matter in a year or more is "no." But when you went for the interview, you were obviously thinking about the long-term life implications of landing the job. Those dreams aren't easily extinguished. It may take some time before you can see the big picture. On the other hand, continuing to play the "if only" game with yourself will inevitably result in a disappointment-depression loop. It's far better to figure out how to move on. And looking at the larger picture may help.

- <u>Remember that success usually comes after many failures.</u>
  Goal: Thomas Edison is often quoted as saying: "*I have not failed. I've just found 10,000 ways that won't work.*" Then there are all of those stories about how many times a manuscript was submitted before it became a bestseller. Or a start-up business that initially lost money but ended up making a bundle. Or athletes who finally reached the top of their game after years of striving to win. The moral? In order to win you have to anticipate failures along the way.

  Challenges: The poster I used to have in my office that said "*If at first you don't succeed, give up*" isn't what most people consider a recipe for success. But the fact that other people had to work hard and face failure before succeeding doesn't guarantee success for anyone else, no matter how hard they try. We know that there are a lot of people who never succeed. Besides, you don't know the end of *your* story yet. If you are going to be one of the success stories, that's one thing–. Still, waiting to have fame thrust upon you won't work either. You have to try in order to achieve. Knowing when to give up or try a new direction may be key to making this tactic work.

- <u>Believe that "everything happens for the best."</u>
  No comment.

- Use positive self-talk to pump up your confidence.
Goal: As most advocates of positive self-talk will tell you, the nega-tive self-talk starts in childhood and increases as our potential fail-ures have larger consequences. If you tell yourself you always fail, or never catch a break, or freeze when under stress, you probably increase your odds of failure. Positive self-talk is a tool that helps you focus on moving forward rather than being driven by the fail-ures of the past.

Challenges: Picture a very young child holding a large ice cream cone, the ice cream already starting to melt, the child eagerly antici-pating the joy to come. The cone wobbles as the small hand tries to maneuver the cone, and you fear that the child is going to turn the cone sideways and the ice cream will fall out. In this situation, most parents will say: *"Don't drop your cone."* Or, *"Be careful."* How much better to be specific, to try to get the child to focus on what CAN be done or explaining what it means to be careful. *"Here, hold the cone in both hands, straight up and down, like this–."* Of course there is still the possibility that the child will tilt the cone and lose the ice cream, but you've tried to teach a long-term lesson instead of simply admonishing the child not to screw up.

Where does positive self-talk end and realistic assessment begin? Sometimes that's difficult to know. You may have to take a step back and ask yourself if there is another way to approach what you are trying to do. Or if there are other options. Through personal experience I have come to believe in the power of positive self-talk, but not as a cure-all.

- Visualize success.
Goal: Many athletes routinely use visualization techniques as part of their training or just before an event. So do actors, speakers – and interviewees. There is considerable research to support the notion

that mental rehearsal can play a powerful role in achieving success. Imagine yourself giving that perfect answer to the request to "tell us a little about yourself." Or, "can you give us an example of a time when…" Picture the approving nods and smiling faces and that feeling of elation for having lived up to your own high standards and hopes.

Challenges: Although there are more advocates for visualization as an effective tool for achieving success than there are detractors, there is some difference of opinion about its uses. For example, a basketball player might visualize making free throws, feeling what it's like to be standing there just before she makes her move, then seeing the ball go through the hoop. That's a very detailed visualization focused on a specific behavior, a moment in time.

But when the outcome isn't as clear cut, the tool may not be as effective. For example, in an interview people may smile at you just because they feel like they should appear to be interested. Or they may frown because they are thinking and analyzing what you said, not necessarily disapproving of anything. In the moment you may not be certain of the outcome, but you will know if you fulfilled your end of the visualization.

Another approach is to visualize a more general success, such as reaching a high-level goal. Creating an "I can do this" attitude. Researchers Kappes and Oettingen [3] make a convincing case that this less detailed visualization may even be counterproductive. They claim that you end up expending the energy that you should be directing toward actually doing something to thinking about doing it. From my point of view, it's like attending a motivational seminar. The impact usually lasts long enough to get you back to your car in

---

3   Heather Barry Kappes and Gabriele Oettingen, "Positive Fantasies About Idealized Futures Sap Energy, *Journal of Experimental Social Psychology* 47 (2011), 719-729.

the parking lot, but not much longer. But then, maybe that's all you will need to get through the interview.

- Plan, plan, plan.
  Goal: In his book, *The Job Search Solution*, Tony Beshara discusses the reasons people don't get the jobs they apply for. He argues that people need to prepare and practice for an interview. He also contends that people need to think about how they can "sell" themselves to a prospective employer. Research the company. Make sure your resume is aligned with the job description. Try to anticipate what questions you will be asked. And make a list of questions you want to ask them. This approach is consistent with one of the Mayo Clinic's suggestions about how to avoid needless stress: They say the key is to "plan ahead."[4] Whether it's stress in general or interview stress, planning is critical. And planning means considering all eventualities.

  Challenges: On the television series, *The A-Team*, Colonel John "Hannibal" Smith always said, *"I love it when a plan comes together."* We all do. But first you have to have a plan. So take Beshara's advice, and plan, plan, plan. Unfortunately, even if you "plan, plan, plan," you must also remember the caveat in the poem by Robert Burns: *"The best laid schemes of mice and men, Often go awry."* So you also need a Plan B.

- Reframe.
  Goal: A frame is a mental model, a way of looking at the world and focusing your attention. Being positive at all costs - is a frame. So is expecting to succeed if you put forth enough effort. And assuming that people get what they deserve. And believing that what goes around comes around. Etcetera. Mental models are the foundation for many of our actions and reactions. They are a mini culture that

---

4   Mayo Clinic website (health information about stress management) at www.mayoclinic.com.

we carry around with us, guiding our behaviors. Being consciously aware of the model allows you to make choices to either accept or reframe how you view something. For example, by reframing how you think about a disastrous interview, you can enhance your understanding of what happened and hopefully find relief. Seeing each interview as a learning experience for instance. Or, as the gist for a story.

Challenges: Reframing can be used to mask reality or to provide camouflage for feelings. It can also be manipulated to serve as a rationalization for failure. That said, it's helpful to think about the assumptions and beliefs that provide the structure for our mental models. We may be holding onto something that isn't (or never was) useful in coping with day-to-day stress. It's like the person who trims the ends off of the ham because grandma always did. Only to find out that Grandma's roasting pan was too small for the hams she had available.

- Laugh.
  Goal: There is a popular saying that "laughter is the best medicine." Some may disagree with the premise, but research has confirmed that laughter can at least be distracting and dull the pain for a while. Perhaps long enough to put your experience in perspective. Long enough to turn it into a story and learning experience for yourself and for others.

  Challenges: As I mentioned above, there is some controversy in the medical field about the positive effects of laughter on health. For example, one researcher found that screaming had some of the same physical benefits as laughter. That reminded me of a woman on my debate team when I was a college debate coach. When she would lose, she would go into the restroom and turn all of the water faucets on to mask the sound — and then she would scream. She claimed that it made her feel better. It probably did. However, it was disconcerting to others trying to use the restroom. A little laughter would have made life easier or all of us.

Conclusion:

When it comes to dealing with stress, you have a wide variety of options to choose from. Finding what works for you takes some trial and error. Obviously, I'm hoping that laughter is part of your solution. Sometimes it takes a while for the laugh to bubble to the surface, but when it does, there are usually beneficial byproducts. Here are some laugh facts:

1. Laughter releases endorphins that result in positive changes in brain chemistry by bringing in more oxygen.
2. Two hormones that suppress the body's immune system – epinephrine and cortisol – drop after a round of laughter.
3. Laughter focuses concentration on coping rather than depression.
4. Simulated laughter has many of the same benefits as real laughter.
5. Children laugh about 200–300 times a day, whereas adults may experience 12-20 laughs.
6. Contrary to the 1998 movie Patch Adams, it isn't necessarily true that clowns improve the quality of life for patients in the hospital. Besides, there is seldom a clown around when you exit from an interview.

This brings me back to the quotation at the beginning of this chapter and the inspiration it provided for the chapter title. I believe it captures the essence of how to cope with disastrous interviews. With laughter. Perhaps not a belly laugh, but at least with an inner chuckle. Otherwise, all you are left with is a bad feeling mixed with regret and the partial satisfaction that at least you aren't the star of a *Groundhog Day* type movie where you have to do more than mentally relive your experience.

Animator Chuck Jones encouraged aspiring professionals to keep drawing by saying: "Every artist has 100,000 bad drawings in him, and the sooner you get through them, the better it is for everybody." The same might be said of interviews. Although, hopefully, getting through other people's bad interviews may suffice. Remember, *it's the laughter that allows hope to creep back on the inhale.*

HR Discussion Guide

Recent surveys by mysteryapplicant.com and Career Builder suggest that between 16 and 25 percent of job applicants have bad experiences with the hiring process. And there is a ripple effect. More than half will tell friends and families about their experience and talk about it via social media. Many will not apply for a job with the company again, some will tell others not to work there, and a few will not purchase products or services from the company. In an ERE.net article, Dr. John Sullivan, professor of management at San Francisco State University, summarizes the consequences in general terms by stating that: "The impact of a poor 'candidate experience' is uncalculated, unreported, and not discussed, making it quite possibly one of the largest 'hidden costs' facing modern organizations."

Conversely, even if they are not hired, candidates who have a positive experience are more likely to apply again, tell others to seek employment there and to purchase the company's products and services. Given these two sets of circumstances, it seems advisable to make an effort to try to avoid making applicants unhappy with the process.

The following questions do not cover all aspects of the interview process; rather, they are linked to the themes that emerged from the interview stories in the book. The goal is to expand on and humanize the lists of recommendations found in books on recruiting, hiring and interviewing by using real-life examples as a starting point for discussion.

1. *I Coulda Been a Contender.* The time employees stay on a job is decreasing while the number of baby boomers retiring is increasing. This will put even more pressure on the hiring process. Do you…

   - *Accept these facts and ramp up your ability to hire more people in less time.* If so, how can you streamline your process? Do you have a 2-3 year plan that is flexible enough to keep up with a rapidly changing workforce?

- *Work on retention strategies.*
Which stakeholders do you need to involve to make this happen? What programs can you create or build on to encourage retention?

- *Both of the above.*
Most staffing plans contain components addressing both of the above, but considering them together encourages a holistic perspective. How do you prioritize actions related to each of these approaches? How do trends outside of your control impact short-term and long-term decisions about staffing?

2. **Humor is Like Pizza.** We know that the saying "laughter is the best medicine" is only partially true. But the ability to laugh at ourselves and at the situations we sometimes find ourselves in can mitigate pain and encourage problem solving by providing perspective.

- Does your team take itself too seriously? What are some ways you can incorporate some fun and laughter into your day-to-day work environment?
- How does your organization respond to mistakes? Is it safe to sometimes "fail" in your culture? What impact does the cultural attitude toward failure have on your team and its working relationships in the organization?
- Does your team create positive stories to reinforce the behaviors they want to see continue?
- In general, does the organization engage in regular activities that encourage having fun together? If not, what kinds of things could you do to promote fun while not distracting from the main goals of the organization?

3. **Culture 2.0.** We all want to hire people that we feel will be a good match for the organization's culture. Candidates understand

that and agree. Everyone wants a "good fit." Unfortunately, many candidates assume that "bad culture fit" is code for "we didn't like you." Some of this may come from how you think about and talk about your culture. Consider whether all of the participants in the interview are on the same page regarding the following questions:

- How do we define our culture?
- How is our culture represented through our brand and online information about the organization?
- What is "culture fit"? What skills and personal characteristics are appropriate for our culture?
- What kinds of questions do we need to ask candidates to determine whether they are a good fit for us?
- What should we say to candidates that we do not hire because of culture fit?
- What do the "lessons learned" from the interview stories tell us about how we can improve our own interview process?

4. **Boobs, Moth Holes and Stray Hairs.** Dress codes are changing. Look around at what members of your team wear to work. What do you notice? Are there unspoken limits of acceptability? Is it different for an interview? Before you make decisions based on appearance, you may want to consider some of the related issues:

- What are some of the assumptions you make about people based on how they dress? Do you consider whether their dress is age appropriate? If so, what does that mean?
- If someone asks about what to wear to the interview, what do you tell them? If you say "business casual," what does that mean to you?
- Do you think women face more challenges when deciding what to wear to an interview than men? What conclusions do you make based on how a woman dresses for an interview?

- Do you have anything on your website about tattoos, facial hair or body piercing? In not, should you?
- Would you eliminate someone for consideration for a position because of a visible tattoo or body piercing? If so, should you give them the option of conforming to company standards?
- Do you assume you can tell how formal or informal they are based on what they wear? How do you think this carries over into the workplace?
- What other assumptions do you make based on appearance?

5. *The Interview Milieu: Misery is Optional.* The interview milieu is a mix of the physical and the social. Although how you treat applicants is crucial, the actual interview setting can have a tremendous impact on how everyone feels about the interview. The first step is to think about what image you want to project. But whether crammed into a tiny space or spread out around a huge table, the amount of influence the setting has can be managed by what – if anything – is said about the setting.

- What does the setting for most of your interviews "say" about how you view the event and the candidate? Is it formal? Informal? Hierarchical? Intended to intimidate to test confidence? Encourage interaction?
- What can you do to put a candidate at ease so you will see them at their best?
- If you do group interviews, are interview team members clear about expectations? Are expectations clearly explained to the candidates? If you withhold information initially to test how candidates deal with uncertainty or vague challenges, at what point do you give them feedback? If you don't give them feedback, what do you think the impact is on their impression of the interview (and of you and your team)?

- Do you believe that challenging interview settings tell you something about the candidate that you cannot learn in a normal setting? If so, test your assumptions by talking about what it is you believe and why you believe it's true.
- How well do you communicate about the process with applicants? Do you let them know what is happening before, during and after the interview?

6. ***Honesty and Other Disasters.*** Some people are adept at positioning the truth, whereas others may be more transparent. There is, however, a difference between "telling it as it is" and choosing what you draw attention to. The classic interview example is asking someone to tell you about their weaknesses. How much "truth" do you expect? The key is to decide in advance what is important to succeed in the particular job and make sure the questions you ask help you identify good candidates.

- Do you ask behavioral questions that tell you enough about past performance to indicate potential for future performance?
- Do you deliberately ask a mix of questions to give you the broadest possible view of the candidate's skills and abilities?
- Do you ask questions about claims made on their resume?
- Is your reference check more than a checkmark?
- If a candidate asks for feedback after the interview, how honest will you be? Do you have a standardized approach for giving post-interview feedback?
- Do you have a plan for evaluating initial on-the-job performance so you can track how effective you are in predicting performance from your interview questions?

7. ***Didn't See That Coming.*** There is no way to anticipate everything that might possibly happen during an interview. Having a consistent process and making sure managers understand their role helps. Also,

having a good set of questions helps. But in the end, you have to be prepared to adapt to whatever comes up in the moment.

- Are all participants in agreement about the process and the questions to be asked? What happens if someone decides to ask something unplanned that is inappropriate? Or just distracting?
- What do you do if it becomes clear that the candidate is not qualified for the position? Do you continue as planned? Do you shorten the interview? How do you maintain process consistency if you change your approach during the interview?
- What are some instances where you have been surprised by either a candidate or one of the interviewers in the past? How was the situation handled? Was it an acceptable outcome?

8. ***Mirth and Missteps.*** Candidates sometimes beat themselves up for perceived mistakes that they make during an interview. But we all make mistakes, including those conducting the interviews. It's how we respond to these mistakes that makes the difference.

- Do you or should you make a decision about a candidate based on one misstep? How accurate do you think you can be about the significance of a pause or a confusing or unfocused response?
- Do you consider the impression you are making on the candidate? Do you discuss image issues with all of the participants in the process?
- If an interviewer asks an inappropriate or illegal question, what do you do?
- Do you demonstrate respect for the candidate? How do you know?
- When you are discussing candidate ratings after the interview, does anyone ridicule a candidate for mistakes made? If so, do you need to do or say something to ensure that cynicism or negativism doesn't become the norm?

9. *No Dead Air in This Interview!* People talk too much for all sorts of reasons – nervousness, the thrill of having a captive audience, for power, or simply because they do not pick up on nonverbal cues.

- If someone comes on a bit too strong from your point of view, what kinds of questions can you ask to determine whether this is a case of nerves or normal behavior? For example, you might simply ask them to tell you how co-workers would rate their enthusiasm for their job and explain the reasons for the rating.
- If a candidate gives long-winded answers, is it your responsibility to let them know that you prefer more brevity? Perhaps you think they should ask if they are providing enough or too much detail. On the other hand, if you ask for a shorter response and they still talk on-and-on, that gives you another piece of evidence for your evaluation.
- What do you do if one of the interviewers starts to dominate the discussion?
- How do you know if *you* are talking too much?

10. *Semper Gumby.* Although being flexible does not guarantee a positive result, consciously choosing when to be flexible and when not to be is usually better than being reactive or rigid.

- To keep the hiring process fair you need to be consistent in your dealings with candidates. Under what conditions would you make an exception? (For example, let's say you are familiar with a candidate – is your interaction with them any different than with the rest of the candidates? How does this impact your decision?)
- In general, how do you balance consistency and flexibility? What exceptions have you made in the past that you've regretted? That you've been pleased that you made? Why?

- If you deviate from the plan, do you later analyze what happened and learn from the experience?

11. **You Think Funny.** Innovation and creativity are valued in today's workplace. And many people think that they can measure someone's ability to be creative by asking some sort of challenging question.

    - Do you want to reward quick thinking or thorough thinking? Which does the job need the most?
    - If someone misunderstands a question, what do you do? a) let them answer and move on, b) stop them in mid-sentence and re-state the question, c) explain after they complete the "wrong" answer that you had actually hoped they would address the issue in a different way, then re-word the question to give them another chance, or d) let them know they didn't give the answer you were expecting and repeat the same question (to keep things fair). What are the pros and cons of each approach?
    - Do you ask some odd questions to test the individual's sense of humor? If so... How important is a sense of humor to the role and to the team? Did nervousness get in the way of the individual's response? Did you consider that linear thinkers laugh at different things than more right-brained individuals?

12. **Spinach in Your Teeth.** How you deal with distractions says a lot about how well you handle uncomfortable situations and whether you show respect for people.

    - For example, when do you tell a person that she has a curler in her hair? If you do so when she first enters the room, it could make her self-conscious. But if you wait until the end of the interview, then she will realize that everyone but her knew it was there the entire time. And, if you don't tell her you noticed the curler, what do you expect her to think or do when she figures it out? Isn't it possible that the person with the curler in her hair is the best candidate for the job? Or does a faux pas like that eliminate her from consideration in your mind? Can you think of any scenario that would cause you to understand and excuse this mistake?

- Have you ever spilled something on yourself right before a meeting where you had to make a presentation? How did you feel? Did you call attention to the stain or try to ignore it? What if you didn't notice until AFTER the meeting? How would you have wanted other people to react?
- Obviously no one intends to be interviewed with their fly unzipped or a button open on their blouse. What is the respectful thing to do or say if you notice something like this?
- Are you aware of the nonverbals related by you and other members of your hiring team? What do they "say" to the candidate? Is this what you want to "say"?

13. *Let's Get Engaged.* We want to feel like candidates are eager to join our particular organization and that they will be engaged and productive employees if hired. We ask questions and try to accurately read nonverbals to determine whether we think the individual will fulfill our expectations.

- True or false: An individual's energy level as displayed during the interview accurately reflects their ability to be engaged in the business of the organization.
- True or false: Millennials and Gen Y candidates can efficiently multi-task, so we should not judge them negatively if they do so during the interview.
- True or false: If someone really wants the job they will do an "ask" at the end of the interview.
- True or false: If they aren't familiar with the company's brand and website, they aren't really interested in the position – they just want a job.

- True or false: What they "say" about their enthusiasm for their work is more accurate than how they "sound" when they talk about it.

14. **The OMG Index.** Common wisdom says that there are many reasons to do some type of group or activity interview, but sometimes those reasons aren't examined carefully in relationship to the job requirements.

- What are the advantages and disadvantages of a panel interview? Is it better used for some positions than for others? Why?
- What is it you believe you can learn from the group interview that you cannot learn in another setting?
- If you use an activity to determine a candidate's ability to do something, how much do you reward speed versus analysis?
- When does it make sense to put a group of candidates through activities together? Is the purpose of the group activity clear? Does it align with what you need to know about the candidates? Do the interviewers know what to look for to evaluate candidates in this setting?
- What kind of feedback do you intend to give participants? Will it be in front of other participants? If so, how do you ensure that it is a positive experience for everyone?

15. **Once Upon an Interview.** Everyone wants a "happy ending," but what's good for the candidate may not be good for you and vice versa. Still, you want people to feel positive about the experience whether they get the job or not.

- Did you make it easy or difficult for the candidate to succeed during the interview? If you introduced challenges or were vague about desired outcomes, what did you do to soften the impact of failure or perceived failure?

- Do you believe that if you tell the candidate too much about what to expect that you don't see the "real" person? Or do you think that clear expectations give the person the opportunity to put their best foot forward? Do some people perform better when things are left vague? Is that the type of person you want to hire? These are all issues that you need to think about in advance to ensure that what you do is consistent with the outcome you are hoping for.

16. *Crème de la Weird.* Sometimes things happen in interviews that cause you to shake your head in disbelief. Because HR is held to a higher standard for confidentiality than other departments, it's wise to be circumspect when talking about the strange things that interviewees do.

- If a candidate's behavior is completely out of the norm, do you let them know that you disapprove or simply cross them off your list? For example, what do you do if someone answers their phone during an interview? Or, what if they say something you consider to be totally inappropriate? Knowing in advance how you want to handle these kinds of situations will help you avoid any complaints that might occur after the fact.
- Do members of the hiring team understand that talking about a weird interview with others could have repercussions? Especially if the story or the timing potentially reveals clues as to the person's identity.

17. *Slacklining: The Art and Science of Interviewing.* There has been a lot of discussion in recent years about the need for HR to be seen as a metrics driven business partner rather than solely as a support function. Making this transition is not easy. People are drawn to HR because they like working with people. The culture is one that usually emphasizes internal customer service and the "soft" issues

associated with managing, nurturing and developing employees. Becoming comfortable with thinking in terms of specific outcomes takes some getting used to.

- What do you measure that directly shows your contribution to the bottom line of the organization? What *could* you measure if you had the tools and resources to do so?
- How satisfied are your internal customers with the metrics associated with the hiring process? Do you provide better service for some areas than for others? If so, how do you account for this? What could you do to improve in the areas that are less satisfied with your services?
- How would you rate the quality of the questions asked during interviews? Do you need to help hiring managers do a better job of creating questions?
- How many "bad hires" do you make that could be avoided by an improved interview process?
- Have you given sufficient thought as to how to recruit and hire across generations?
- Do you need to make changes in what you do to retain younger employees?

18. *The Inhale.* You can never completely eliminate stress, but there are tools that help you cope with and reduce stress levels. The premise of this book is that one of the main tools is to turn bad experiences into stories that put the experience in perspective and enable you to laugh at what happened.

- Do you routinely check with team members about job pressures and stress?
- Do people pay lip service to being "stressed out" or do they accurately assess the role stress plays in their day-to-day performance?

- Are there stress reduction options the entire team can participate in?
- What stress reduction techniques and tools seem the most appropriate for individual team members?
- What kinds of things add to the stress of team members? Can any of these be eliminated or reduced?

Conclusion:

There are companies that specialize in making recruiting and hiring programs highly sophisticated and efficient. You can spend a ton of money to update and streamline your system. But when you read about candidate complaints, it usually comes down to very human issues – keeping candidates informed, making sure the job description matches what is presented in the interview, and being treated respectfully. One final suggestion: it's a good idea to routinely survey candidates to get feedback on ways you can improve the process for everyone involved.

Made in the USA
San Bernardino, CA
29 December 2013